WANTED

*From Child Homelessness to a Death-Defying
Search for Love and Belonging*

WANTED

*From Child Homelessness to a Death-Defying
Search for Love and Belonging*

MAT BUNCH WITH CANDI S. CROSS

Early Praise

"We all have struggles in life and stories to tell. For some, those struggles seem to compound and can break the strongest of spirits. So, when a story of resilience and determination emerges, we are all drawn to it. That is the story of Mat Bunch. But he goes beyond his personal story to draw us in and motivate us to action. You will walk away happy, sad, satisfied, and rededicated."

—*Todd A. Weiler, Former Asst. Secretary of Defense, Author of Untamed Equality*

"*Wanted* is both gritty and dreamy, showing us what is humanly possible in this life even as we encounter all kinds of monsters. And it just so happens to come with a playbook on how to change the world in the most deliberate ways. Thank you, Mat!"

—*Christopher Gasti, Stage and Screen Actor, Advocate, Author of The Show Must Go On*

"Mat's story goes from heart-wrenching, depicting how addiction and abuse damage children, to heart-throbbing for those of us lucky enough to find the partner of our dreams, to heart-centered in the actions we should all commit to for the health and wellbeing of the planet. *Wanted* moves and motivates start to finish."

–DAVID CARLUCCI, FORMER NEW YORK STATE
SENATOR, AUTHOR OF DISRUPTIVE RESULTS

"If a book is designed to make you think and feel, Mat Bunch's *Wanted* is the full package of our human experience. Sometimes it's not pretty but turning away robs us of courage and insight. We are reminded there is no greater need than to belong. Mat is victorious, perceptive, and sharply relevant on his mission to help others achieve what he did from rock bottom."

—ALINA LEE, ATTORNEY AND AUTHOR

"Every individual's life has meaning; every individual has worth. Cast aside and abused, Mat Bunch early life was one of basic survival and a struggle to overcome unimaginable challenges. His life story now gives hope to humanity that life has meaning and worth as he helps to save the world for all of us and more importantly, those who will follow us."

—GREG MORLEY (HE/HIM/HIS), REGIONAL DIRECTOR
HUMAN RESOURCES ASIA OCEANIA/GLOBAL HEAD OF
DIVERSITY, EQUITY AND INCLUSION, MOËT HENNESSY

"*Wanted* is an open letter to the world on the power of hope. Mat Bunch allows us VIP access into his life, his thoughts, and his journey to find the love he knows exists and teaches us so much about ourselves and the world along the way. Wanted is real, bold, and necessary to the contemporary leadership narrative, and we are grateful to Mat for trusting us with his story!"

—MARY MICHELLE HEMPHILL, PH.D., ADJUNCT INSTRUCTOR, MPA PROGRAM, UNC SCHOOL OF GOVERNMENT

"*Wanted* is an uncomfortable reminder that we do not all have the luxury of being wanted. Mat has risen like a beautiful phoenix. Dreaming is very important to me, and Mat has demonstrated he lives the dream he envisions."

—TRACE SHERER, RETIRED ATTORNEY AND MEDIATOR, AUTHOR OF NERVES OF STEEL

"*Wanted* focuses the mind to the chain of abuse that we collectively participate in by turning away, rushing by, minding our own business, and the corrosion of one's soul of not caring."

—MARCIA ELIZABETH CHRISTIAN FAVALE, FOUNDER AND CEO, BLINGBY

"In vivid detail, Mat's story exposes the epic failure of the rickety systems in place to 'protect' the most vulnerable. But he rose up to persevere and be a powerful force for change. Mat wasn't just a little gay boy trying to survive. At the age of six, he kept his own mother alive! And his forgiving, cause-oriented approach to life is beyond inspirational. Do not only skim this book for you might miss a nugget that you need at this very moment."

—*Irene Brank, Transgender Workplace Consultant and Gender Transition Partner*

"Mat Bunch invites the reader into his most vulnerable parts and makes them feel wanted. You'll not only take in the words but the urgency that lingers in such merciless details and merciful forgiveness. He is an inspiration to not only all who identify as LGBTQ+, but also, to all people who aspire to manifesting their vision."

—*Fiona Dawson (she/her), Founder & Director, Free Lion Productions*

"Mat's story cuts like a knife and attempts to heal just as rapidly. He confronts multiple enemies of a fair, just world while serving up a generous offering of hope for tomorrow. *Wanted* is a modern memoir that makes you question if you are doing enough. So, are you?"

—*Eric Alva, Retired Marine Staff Sergeant, Author of Radical Courage*

"*Wanted* does more than tell the story of someone who spent his childhood and much of his adult life searching for love and belonging. It brings to light just how damaging it is when we don't see beyond someone's hardships. The discomfort you feel as you take in the reality lived by Mat Bunch is the kind of discomfort that proceeds a growth that allows for more compassion towards others. There is something special in the way he writes, it makes you an active reader."

—Antuan Magic Raimone, TEDx Speaker, Author of
Becoming Magic: A Path of Personal Reconstruction

Contents

Acknowledgments

Foremost, I am honored to humbly acknowledge all the members of my *chosen family* who have acted as my conscience and guiding light and throughout my life, from serving as parental figures, siblings, aunts, and uncles, to my best friends and dear mentors. Also, I would not be the person today without my husband, Matt, and our beautiful family. Without his love and support–from first encouraging me to write this memoir to reviewing early drafts and our late-night copyediting sessions–I may not have ever had the courage to be vulnerable enough to share my story.

My sincerest gratitude to my co-author, Candi Cross, who helped me understand telling my story is a responsibility I have to everyone out there who has ever felt as though they did not belong. For helping me put some of the most difficult aspects of my story on paper. And for inspiring me to be a better writer, storyteller, and author.

I would undoubtedly not be who I am today without my childhood social worker and lifetime friend, Beth, the first person to truly believe in me and my true self. I dedicate this book to her. She showed me from an early age that that love is possible as long as you open up your heart: that love comes not always from your bloodline but from a strong connection, caring, and mutual support. I hope every foster child can find their "Beth," that person whose unequivocable belief in you feels as genuine as a parent, and that spark of belief—of true care and compassion—opens an entire world of finding and accepting love, belonging, and most importantly, accepting yourself.

Finally, I am immensely grateful for my readers: my hope is that you will gain some nugget of inspiration from one of the principles of my story; that your God-given circumstances don't have to determine your final fate, no matter your socioeconomic or family status. That no matter how dark times may be, give yourself permission to feel Wanted. You deserve it. Believe in yourself—I believe in you.

Introduction

Early Education in Love and Belonging

> "When you get to a place where you understand that
> love and belonging, your worthiness, is a birthright and
> not something you have to earn, anything is possible."
>
> —*Brené Brown*,
> *research professor and author*

Do you ever think of childhood and pull up a story or image that makes you smile?

I am still trying to find that one sunken treasure in the children's section of the library of my mind. In the adulthood section, wow, I have endless capers, magical moments, adventures, blessings, to curl up to.

My memories of childhood are more like shards of glass than anything flowery or soothing. These shards have helped to define me as a man, as a husband, as a friend, and as a leader. My journey to love and belonging was extremely windy. I share it with you, not only to educate and inspire but also, to encourage you to own your whole story and use it as a source of strength.

I vividly remember being evicted. I remember sleeping in the back of a truck with a small covering over the bed for weeks, if not months. My mother could not take care of me, so I took care of the both of us—from gathering food, to washing my own clothes in the sinks at school. We didn't have a home, so she found a woman at work who was willing to take me in—not out of love and belonging but for a check. My mother had no way of knowing the hell I would go through. Before she sold me, it seemed like we would have been living in the back of that truck until someone just pushed us off another cliff.

We were outcasts, alone, living on the fringes in rural Indiana. No one would have paid attention to our disappearance. At the age of six, I remember thinking, *we don't belong anywhere*. No one wanted us, so we needed to hang on to each other with every breath. These are some, though not all, of my earliest memories.

For my newly widowed mother to make the decision to sell me, I've now realized that it was the best decision she could make as a mom addicted to alcohol or drugs. It makes no difference how much this is still being debated: alcoholism, or any addiction, is a mental health issue that impairs brain function. My mom was sick. In addition to being addicted, she suffered from severe anxiety and depression; I, too, live and struggle with both mental health challenges. Regardless, she shouldn't have been in the position to make these decisions. She barely had a mind left after drinking herself into oblivion every single day, despite six-year-old me trying my damnedest to keep both of us alive.

Since these days living in the truck and the day she abandoned me, I have greatly contemplated what being *wanted* means and then chasing this permanent embrace at all costs. I've also studied the behavior in others who never fully feel solid in that they do belong somewhere, that they matter to someone, and that they are loved.

These are basic requirements for a young person's roots to grow deep and prepare them for life ahead.

Suffering from extreme physical and emotional abuse is what defined the next seven years of my life. Constantly under physical assault resulting in bruises, pain, and fear, coupled with being called "fat" and "gay" slurs at such an impressionable age (especially by my new "legal guardian," nonetheless), made me feel isolated from other children that were "wanted." I know I, and a lot of adolescents, take comments about weight and appearance deeply personally, struggling to reconcile this throughout life. I still find myself struggling with body image issues and self-consciousness, regardless of how healthy I may appear to others.

Homeless and hungry, I survived on the instincts I had. I lived by this mantra: that I was worthy of love and belonging, despite the dark times when it didn't feel that way. Although my brain was only six years old, I knew then that *every* child is worthy. I bounced between several foster homes, an orphanage, and eventually breaking out of the Indiana foster care system, convincing a judge I'd be better off living on my own as a junior in high school. Somehow, I never gave up on my quest for self-discovery nor on my belief that I was worthy of love. I never stopped espousing as much loving kindness and passion to everyone I possibly could in this world, and I somehow knew—even throughout my childhood—that I would someday be the recipient of that same cosmic love.

This quest to be wanted has materialized in every facet of my life.

It's not that I couldn't ever face rejection or emotional pain. I did: a lot and often intensely. Sometimes I survived on pure instinct. Sometimes I even sang my way through it! For me, what I am speaking of has a deeper meaning. I hope to inspire others who have been marginalized, who have ever felt helpless in their lives or suffered child abuse or homelessness. I want all children to know that their socioeconomic circumstances and trauma may have a permanently detrimental impact, but that they can still achieve their dreams. This often begins with teenagers truly *believing* they, too, can at least have access to the opportunities of college education, trade school, and training as a foundation of achieving the life they perhaps only dreamed about before this realization.

I survived a life of homelessness, pain, loss, abuse, and rejection. Despite the trauma, I kept faith that one day I, too, would feel worthy of love and belonging—that I could even feel wanted someday. This is my story.

CHAPTER 1
A Glimmer of Stability

"My life is a beautiful struggle."

—*Hope Solo, champion soccer goalkeeper*

BORN IN CONSERVATIVE rural Indiana, my life may have started off like a seemingly normal young boy. A stable home, loving father and mother, middle-class resources. The first few years of my life, from what I remember, were a glimmer of what a normal life might be. My story begins with my father.

James, a veteran from the U.S. Army, was older than my mom, born in the 1930s or 1940s. He was our rock. He began teaching me to read and write almost as soon as I had learned to speak. I still remember the look on his face when I read my first book aloud, *Green Eggs and Ham*. He and my mom were so proud, they finally purchased the brand-new *National Geographic* encyclopedias I so persistently begged for every time the commercial came on TV. He kept us safe, housed, and fed. Up until his very last breath.

I remember my father being very stoic. I only remember the

image of one family portrait, one photograph of us together, from Olan Mills. When tragedy strikes or trauma sets in, you forget what is normal, or maybe you don't have any feeling for it at all. I do remember at age five, though, living in a neighborhood where we assembled a treehouse for the kids so large that it stretched halfway into the neighbors' back yard. I remember using that treehouse to escape home life. I knew something was different about me. I remember feeling ashamed that I didn't like girls. I liked boys. It wasn't a matter of "sexuality" at that age; I just knew very early in my life that I had to conceal the fact that I would never be "normal" with a wife and kids someday. I was never myself with my parents, but I didn't feel the same pressure to pretend or gloss over any trait with my friends. We had so much fun in that stylish treehouse with never-ending branches extending out, emulating a monster outside my bedroom window in the middle of the night. When we had lights installed in the treehouse, I would even take my sleeping bag out at night where I could be alone by myself, the only time I truly felt wanted, warm and safely cocooned inside the tree's branches. At this moment in my life, though family life seemed rosy, I was already experiencing what it meant to feel outcast. At this moment, a treehouse was certainly not the worst place to be exiled.

We were fortunate to possess the resources to have a house and a community. I was very social. If the phone rang, I popped up like a jack-in-the-box, expecting one of many friends to call. Oh, the days before screen time—when everybody in the house had to share the same land line! I always spoke up in class and made teachers laugh. We went fishing almost every weekend, which was generally fun except for the slimy earthworms I didn't want to touch. My mom would hook the bait for my line, every time. I walked around singing at the top of my lungs, full of energy and ever curious. I was aware my mom was a heavy drinker; my dad was steadily a good influence on her, so most times, she'd sober up under his watchful eye for me.

Then that dreadful day came.

One cool, spring night, while my mother was passed out in another alcohol-induced coma, I knew, even as a kindergartener, to call 9-1-1 as I saw my dad drop to the floor in front of me, dead from heart attack. I didn't freeze. I instinctively ran over to him. But it was too late.

The next few days, his funeral…the memories are a blur. I vaguely remember being sad, mostly because everyone else looked sad. And mom was so angry for someone to blame; she looked to me: "You didn't call 9-1-1 fast enough, so he died." This created a guilt I'd end up harboring most of my life, despite coming to understand I was not to blame. But at the age of six, does anyone truly comprehend death? This was, though, the beginning of a period of damaging behavior from my mom. The man was barely dead, but in a rapid turn of events, she decided to tell me that my dad, James, was not even my real dad anyway. I later learned that I do not have a legitimate father on my birth certificate.

In the early days after his passing, I remember cooking a super-duper grilled cheese made of Velveeta and ground beef as she delivered this information that I didn't have the maturity to process. Of course, she delivered this news while polishing off another bottle of wine. Looking back, the irony in this moment is that I learned how to cook basic meals before some kids master the basics of reading. I remember the fear this moment invoked inside me. Our protector was no longer here to save her, let alone me. This is one of the first memories I have of her beginning to spiral out of control.

CHAPTER 2

From Home to Homeless

"Home is a notion that only nations of the homeless
fully appreciate and only the uprooted comprehend."

— WALLACE STEGNER,
ENVIRONMENTALIST AND NOVELIST

WE LOST THE house. I still feel like I lost my "home" when my father died. The two events happened in quick succession.

I remember Mom, stone cold, as we clumsily moved some items into the truck. No boxes. A potpourri of things that held little meaning. Then my mind races ahead, my next memory of eating soup out of a can, looking down at my dirty fingers as I used the lid as a makeshift spoon.

Where is my mother in this snapshot?

She is snoring and drooling from a dark liquid that smells foul. It was alcohol. This scent, this image, and this habit becomes a daily occurrence for months.

When I was older, in my twenties, the funeral director told me that James, my "dad," had died by suicide, that he had taken too many pills, which led to the heart attack. To this day, I have no idea whom to believe. If it is true that my "dad" committed suicide and my mom couldn't deal with that, her addiction could be more justified, and *that* is what caused the homelessness. To a child who lost his father, death and abandonment may look the same (you'll never see the person again), but they are not the same. They have different consequences on a child, especially if that death results in the loss of stability and the advent of abuse or neglect. With the other parent lost in her own oblivion, this means both my parents effectively "left." No matter the cause of his death, the effect on my mother eventually led her into this downward spiral that I could not understand. But deep down, I always knew that we deserved better. I would settle for nothing less, and I have never stopped fighting for the betterment of those in my life.

I do remember teachers asking me where my mom was. My answers were always vague. Deep down, I knew our situation wasn't right. I was worried about my mother drowning in her own vomit, but as much as I wanted to ask for help, I didn't want to lose her, too.

I was a smart, resourceful kid from an early age. I was disciplined enough to get out of a makeshift "bed," a dirty mattress placed in bed of that truck, and make it on time for school, get myself to school, and then get back to make sure the only person in the world who mattered (and to whom I still mattered) was breathing. I believe that daylight may have served as my clock for what to do and when to do it.

We had no money, but I did my best to feed and take care of us. I found a way to convince the owner of the local Village Pantry to permit me to take some expired food items home on my walk from school, and I'd stop by most days to grab the expired canned goods. We had an electric plate that I was at least able to plug into the cigarette lighter to use as a makeshift stove range. The irony again: she had taught me how to cook because I was so particular about my food. Now, this skill was a necessity to keep us alive.

Not only was I harboring the secret about who I truly was at home; I worked my hardest to conceal being known as the "poor, homeless, gay kid" to my friends and teachers. Despite my best effort, the school finally figured out I was homeless, in the same clothes and obviously without a bath or shower. While my situation finally mattered to one of my teachers, the tormenting of the other kids for wearing the same few clothes, day after day for months, certainly made me feel unworthy and unwanted.

One day, my teacher suspected something. She tried to walk me home. I jumped up and shouted, "No, I'm fine!" She stood there with a frown and watched me walk down the sidewalk. We were living on the edge, not sure who would fall off first or if we would plunge to our death together.

After all the suspicion from my school, my mom decided to leave me with her old coworker and her three kids for a weekend. I was just so relieved to be in a house with rooms and a roof again, not worrying about my next meal or shower. Her daughters and I hit it off to start with—we would play with Barbie dolls and the Easy Bake Oven. Then, out of nowhere, my mom asked me if I wanted to live with this woman. Sure, I didn't feel so vulnerable for the first time in many months, and "yes" came easy and somewhat unintentionally or unknowingly. The way it was explained to me was that this mysterious woman, who didn't show any disquieting signs and whom my mother trusted with her kid, was going to be my "godmother." I didn't know I wouldn't see my mom again.

CHAPTER 3

It's Going Dark Now but Not Forever

"We think sometimes that poverty is only being hungry, naked, and homeless. The poverty of being unwanted, unloved, and uncared for is the greatest poverty. We must start in our own homes to remedy this kind of poverty."

—MOTHER TERESA, MISSIONARY

IT'S SAFE TO say, we must continue to examine the psychological effects of these events on children to give them the proper tools for their psychological and emotional growth. It took me fifteen years to learn enough, to understand enough, to move on from much of the pain.

Emotions play a significant role in making and storing memories. On any given day, our brains store or "encode" only *some* of the things we experience, as reported by a piece for NPR. "What we pay attention to is what's more likely to get encoded," said Jim Hopper, a teaching associate in psychology at Harvard University and a consultant on sexual assault and trauma. In fact, a region of the brain called the *hippocampus* plays an important role in this process. "The hippocampus certainly plays a role in taking things into short-term memory and then transferring them and consolidating them into long-term memories," says Hopper. If an event elicits an emotional reaction in us, then it's more likely to make it into our memory. "Things that have more emotional significance tend to get more encoded," he says. And when something elicits an intense negative emotion, like a trauma, it's even more likely to be encoded in the brain.

"The stress hormones, cortisol, norepinephrine, that are released during a terrifying trauma tend to render the experience vivid and memorable, especially the central aspect, the most meaningful aspects of the experience for the victim," says Richard McNally, a psychologist at Harvard University and the author of the book, *Remembering Trauma*.

Up until now, I certainly experienced pain. Sadness. Uncertainty. But except for watching my dad pass, I clearly had few memories I encoded for the long term; however, this is where my story turns toward real trauma.

These events I remember in vivid detail.

This was when the darkness started to fall.

When I first arrived at "Connie's" house, things initially felt like they were going to be better. Then…abandonment. My mom decided to abandon me, essentially selling me to Connie, who took me because of the significant money she would receive from my dad's veteran benefits that my mom could offer her. At the time, I did not realize what was going on. I was excited. I felt like I would have three sisters and a mom who was at least alert and awake. I had a bed again. I had a real fork and spoon. No more rusty soup can lids.

As the days passed and my mom never returned, it became clear that this was more of a permanent situation.

Connie was working in a restaurant as a single parent with four kids. She was also going through a divorce from an abusive husband. I suppose one day she just erupted, as we were arguing about something, and she pushed me down the stairs. While I cried and screamed for my "real" mother, she knocked me down the stairs like a hysterical animal, hitting and punching me. I covered my face.

For days, I only slept in patches. All I did was re-imagine every tumble.

Every punch.

Every cry for my mom, who never answered those cries.

Every memory like this getting coded into my brain long-term.

After a while, many incidents such as these piled up high, collecting dust almost like old magazine editions never read. The difference is that you may legitimately forget what articles you save the magazine edition for in the first place. Your body does not forget traumatic events. With each flurry of emotions, my mind registered these events, encoding them in my brain. When I started seeing a therapist many years later, the psychologists said, "They are burned in your brain because of the emotional context." At this point, the assaults took on two different types of memories for me. I remember some of the *physical* pain since I can still recall memories like flashbacks to specific moments of abuse. For me, the harder memories were the *emotional* ones. Being called names. Cooking and cleaning after her and her three girls. Longing for my mom. Desiring to be anywhere else in the world. Wishing to be loved.

I never hit back. Somehow, I knew better. I never struck Connie with my hands, mostly because my hands were usually trying to cover my own face and body. If she were on top of me, I would try to kick her away. I was never the aggressor, as I would never do anything to put myself back on the street, alone. That fear of homelessness and loneliness was worse to me than my fear of being beaten. She would show people bruises on her own arms and claim that I was abusing her. Meanwhile, she regularly covered me up with cakes of makeup and big Band-Aids on my body and face to cover the bruises. These very words defied the type of kid I was—through all of this, I remained lighthearted, personable, and passionate in everything I did.

A long, agonizing year passed in this house. Then one day, out of the blue, my mom showed up at Connie's. When she returned, I told her about the abuse and when it began. I'm not sure if she legitimately wanted me back to protect and save me or if she was simply concocting a way to begin receiving my dad's veteran money again. However, she indeed, "wanted me back" and proceeded to fight in court for custody. Regardless, it all felt transactional; I did not feel wanted.

Connie, the monster-mom, fought my own mother for me. The court awarded a series of home visits, overnight, with my mom. I remember the first night playing Tetris and watching "The Golden Girls" together like we used to. But in the repetitive cycle that can be alcoholism, my mom got slapped with a DUI on the second night of our home visit while I was sleeping. I was sent back to the well-paid legal guardian for $2,400 a month between my dad's benefits and her existing state- and federal-provided care—a fortune for rural Indiana, especially when you're dealing drugs, receiving welfare benefits, and living in federal housing.

I came to learn that during that year, my mom was not dead, nor was she homeless. She was living with a different man every few months. None of these men wanted to stay with us, as it wasn't worth it to them to masquerade as a father figure to me to have her. She may have been going through a period of remorse or singlehood during that time, but whatever that year was for her, she hadn't developed enough strength or resolve to get me back. After a year of Connie's abuse, I was able to have one night with Mom before the police took me back to Connie's. I never saw my mother again. This meant six more years charred with abuse.

One of the worst memories I can recall is being tied up in the basement and held down by two 200-pound men, as if they were her bodyguards warding off another grown man, while she beat me. What was going on in my mind being held captive in a chair for almost forty-eight hours? I was scared. I was starving, although I could not stomach the idea of food. I wanted my mom and dad. I felt I would never escape. If I cried or yelled, she would come down and continue the abuse. So, for every one of those hours, I sobbed quietly: wishing, hoping, and praying to God that I would be freed from this captivity or at least be given a meal. It was a depraved cycle that had no rhyme or reason other than the fact that my sick mother had left me with an even sicker—in fact, soulless—woman. Being tied down, being starved, serving as a child slave cleaning the three bedrooms of the girls, the bathrooms, and the kitchen every day.

During the summers, I witnessed Connie dealing and using more and more drugs. Those same "bodyguards" and even more strange men came to the house more regularly. If the whole house was not clean—spotless—she would beat me to the ground even after finding one speck of dust. Essentially living as an abused child slave, even today, my mind flashes back to those days when thinking about cleaning a mere dish, sliding into the depths of anxiety and depression. A lasting, crippling affect for many years; in fact, most of my life up to age twenty.

I vividly recall one time, about a year after my mother disappeared, Connie was applying for housing assistance. To qualify, the house needed to have fewer than four bedrooms. To the state at the time, a room was only considered a "bedroom" if it included a closet. I remember the pride I had after suggesting that if we got some wood panels, we could hide the closet. The scheme worked! After inspection, the house was considered a three-bedroom rather than a four-bedroom. With my idea at play, Connie received free housing from HUD.

That night, I asked, "Aren't you proud of me?"

Her words were terse, calling me "worthless," striking me again for talking out of turn. Even though I knew it would likely end in a bloody fight, I had enough of her manipulation: I bolstered the courage to call her "ungrateful" for my help with the house, which inflamed her even more. The night ended with a punch in the face and her screaming, "On the wall, boy!" Seven hours standing upright in the corner with a black eye emerging, a belt-whipping to my legs and back with even the slightest slouch.

The next day, I took my usual two-block walk to school, with makeup covering my face. This was one of many times Connie would use her daughters to torment me. In between the time I left the house and made it to school, her daughters started telling kids and teachers that I was physically abusive toward *them*. They were turning out to be confused pawns in this woman's sick, twisted game. This happened on several occasions where she would convince the girls to lie about something, even lie to teachers about why I would have bruises. After actively turning them against me, one of the girls who was my age was held back in school. While she was thirteen days older than me, she was now a grade behind. This is a jealousy she'd never let me forget. She hurt herself on the playground that day at school and told Connie that I did it. In sheer avoidance, they grew to see their mother "defending herself" as if I were the aggressive one, but I was the only one she abused; the three of them simply watched—the oldest even helping her hold me down. This was when I began to realize Connie was not a mere evil person; she was disturbed. Somehow, I knew that while I desired to be wanted or loved, deep down I was glad it wasn't by someone like her.

I faced fire a few times. I remember smelling the burning flesh, which is very distinct and stays with you like the battle scars on my arms and legs do. The flames of abuse only intensified. During one of her episodes after a drug deal, Connie almost wrecked her car into a ditch/river threatening to kill us both, flying down a winding country road at what felt like ninety miles an hour, by lakes and across bridges. I wasn't sure what would be worse: fire or drowning.

Alas, we would always remain back at the house with a revolving door of men coming in and out. She would always find new reasons to "punish" me, no matter how much I obeyed her commands.

One random day, the second man, whom my mother claimed was my father, bought me a bike for "good grades." I was thrilled since the girls always had bikes (and the irony of them telling the school that my bruises resulting from "falling off my bike"). Of course, instead of building my confidence and self-esteem or supporting me, Connie told me the only reason was that when I got older, he was afraid I was going to kill him once I became an "angry teen" for being such a terrible father: that he would never love a sick child like me and wouldn't take me out of her home and care for me. Another sick game to entice the victim, a now ten-year-old, to somehow believe I deserved the abuse.

She slowly became rasher and more abusive physically and emotionally. In the years since, I have learned more about perhaps why she treated me the way she did. She, herself, was a victim of abuse by many older men. Once she divorced her last batterer, she became the batterer. I think she felt empowered. I was a child, not yet even a teenager. She knew she could overpower me. She thought she could keep covering it up. There was no way she could lose.

There were many days when she would work very hard to pretend everything was normal at home, even between us. For example, she wanted me to watch TV shows with her, curled up on the couch like her buddy or furry pet. I never once felt like I belonged there as a son or loved one. It never felt like family time. This notion of family time curled up in front of the TV commiserating with a hero or villain and cuddling someone who was not threatening bloomed as a fantasy in my mind. Didn't every family or couple watch movies together? Oddly enough, Connie never chummed up like that with her daughters. For a fleeting moment, I would hope things might be different, then the next thing you know, I faced her closed fists again.

It was a morbid game of cyclical abuse: nearly every time these traumatic events happened over those long seven years, she would then cry and hug me afterwards, releasing either tears of regret or self-deprecation, whispering promises this would be "the last time." We cried together. She would say sorry. I felt sorry for her, I believed her. I would then beg her not to hurt me again, every time. I had been tricked into believing her apologies and promises to stop; perhaps this very belief is what kept me from getting in trouble throughout adolescence against all odds, despite my home conditions? It was clear she knew my dad's veteran check would be at risk if the authorities found out. She plastered makeup on me so no one could see the bruises and open wounds, and then she even called me "gay" in front everyone for wearing makeup, the makeup she put on me. Maybe she wanted to drive me insane so I could join her in psychological melee. I still knew never to hit her back.

I feel sorry for Connie. It is natural for me to think of others' experiences and wellbeing. At the same time, the older I got while under her care, the more determined I became to grow up to be a rock star, to realize every dream I could, despite that every single day spent with this woman was one where she would tear me down, calling me "nothing," a meaningless object to defile. A child that not even God would love. When I whispered, "I forgive you," it must have been more profound than merely believing she was sorry. Some may say I was soft-hearted, but the alternative—turning my heart off, turning it cold and ironclad—might as well have been death. For many abuse victims, that's the only answer, which effectively becomes a life prison. I am not precisely sure why I chose the forgiveness path before I understood what forgiveness meant. Maybe instinct. I knew early on that I did matter and that someone would love me. I also did it for practical reasons, as she was a large adult wielding power. I am grateful that by the time I found love, I could have unwittingly closed the door of my heart, rendering myself unable to receive love or believe I was worthy of being loved.

CHAPTER 4
Singing for Survival

"Music is moonlight in the gloomy night of life."

—*Jean Paul, author*

"Eat another Twinkie, fat ass!" I can still hear her shrill voice after I came home from school beaming with pride, joy, and excitement. I had made the show choir's biggest production of the year and landed a lead solo. Anything to do with the arts was lost on this household, so I wasn't exactly expecting to be showered with praise. But with this news that could set the course for my future, Connie increased the volume of insults. And I was not obese—just growing!

No one should be called names like this, especially not kids. In an ideal world, no one's ears would have to hear such negative language since words matter so much. During a child's most formative years, the ego is so easily and permanently influenced by the words people say around you. Words make dents in your personality, whether they are true or not; you can't discern the difference as a kid. I struggle today with body image issues, and my earliest memories of developing these insecurities were with Connie.

I was so proud. I landed the star role in the Christmas play. From my early memories singing around the house with my mom and dad to this moment, this was the first time in a long time I truly felt wanted: there was even an audition! And they picked *me*! It did not matter that the subject was Christmas; my memories of Christmas after losing my parents were unpleasant. One Christmas, Connie wrapped separate socks to make it look like I had multiple presents in case a nosy social worker or any gossipy type in rural Indiana banged on the door. The girls would get electronics and CDs, and once, they even got a cell phone. I never had the luxury of being materialistic, but this always made me feel like an outcast. Going to school, all the kids would be talking about what they got, big or small.

Connie would repeatedly tell me that no one would want to see me in that play because I was "too fat." After walking nearly two miles to show choir practice for months, every day, and sometimes even after taking physical blows from my guardian, Connie dropped the bomb on me. Late afternoon of the performance, as I stepped out of the shower, she declared, "You're not going."

I begged, cried, and my screams were probably louder than a blue whale, but Connie wouldn't let me go to the Christmas show. She didn't care that I had the star role. The whole school hated me for this. It was as if I had deliberately blown off a major production and shorted all the other kids waiting for their big night. She made sure that I couldn't feel success or feel pride. At the same time, because of her actions, the entire staff at school, and even some of my closest friends, thought that *I* was a manipulative, lying monster who faked this abuse for mere attention.

Right after that dark night, multiple kids and even the teachers scoffed at me because of the failed musical. Soon thereafter, a basketball star looked me up and down during lunch as though I were some foul troll and asked me why I spent my time singing and not playing sports. Even then, I knew I would never be the jock type. Music was my support system. I needed singing. It's all I had to myself. I knew I was talented, even when Connie kept me from showing it sometimes.

Once I entered the seventh grade, I made it to boys' choir. Being part of a group for the first time, the Middle School Chorale, helped me to persevere in academics. Inclusion is real in middle school years, significantly relating to self-esteem, acceptance, and positive interpersonal relationships. This sense of belonging at school made me more resilient in Connie's lair where I had to face dragons. Encouraging kids to pursue their bliss, be it music, sports, dance, art, science—whatever—rather than silencing that inner talent, inner expression, is a major predictor in their self-esteem as an adult and their ability to persevere. Music, for me, was lifesaving. It was my only place to grow, to build friendships, to garner praise, build my confidence. Music helped me to believe I somehow would rise above and escape this hell hole.

CHAPTER 5

Lost in the Foster Care System

"It is easier to build strong children
than to repair broken men."

—*Frederick Douglass, abolitionist*

It's not breaking news. Some people take in foster children solely for the money. You don't pay for healthcare. You also receive food stamps. That was, in the end, the reason Connie "took care" of me, banking on that check, a significant money payout she would receive from my dad's veteran benefits that my mom could offer her.

I always felt *sold*. What does this feel like as a child? Like you are a discarded object, with no inherent value of your own and only valuable because of the money itself; since you don't have a good reference for relationships, it leaves you vulnerable and operating by pure instinct, not emotional experience nor maturity. No one looked for me. I was in the same school system in New Castle, where I had made many friends and pretended to be happy in front of them and my teachers.

The foster care system in Indiana is so closely tied to religion, forcing you to convert to Christianity, or claim to be Christian, in exchange for basic needs to be met by the resources the religion-based organizations provide. Adults benefitting and children enmeshed in this system do not have a choice of exercising their fundamental beliefs. In addition, at least in "my day," church service was free childcare for some of my foster parents. I always imagined growing up one day and discovering God on my own terms and beliefs. Thankfully, that quest has materialized.

After the Christmas musical incident where Connie forbade me to go and perform the solo in third grade, time wore on like an abscessed tooth threatening to explode. Every night, as part of a new punishment method, I would have to stand in the corner for hours, absolutely *no* slouching, listening to one episode of "Maury Povich" after another while everyone else was on the couch lounging. It was like public humiliation. Then all the laundry. More labor, but just for me. Never for her daughters.

By seventh grade, Connie pulled me out of all my music, one of the few aspects of life that gave me joy. I think this was the last straw of abuse. I could take the physical pain, but I was empty without singing. Indeed, I had immersed myself in everything that the school offered, excelling in regular classes and other extracurricular activities.

When I finally summoned enough courage to risk it all, my future safety and possibly my life, I told an adult, yet again, and with more vivid detail. I had told someone about this rampant abuse four times before. Each time, I held back. I did not give a lot of detail because I knew, deep down, that if Connie were to find out and I was not removed from her custody, the pain and abuse would get worse. That fear was immobilizing. It traps you. You know what the abuser is capable of, and fear of death trumps fear of abuse. This time, I didn't hold back. Both the teacher and the case worker, again, thought I was making up my story, "because you are an orphan."

I cannot convey the shock I felt from being accused of lying about the abuse that I ultimately became brave enough to speak of. Now, I was forced into utter fear of tumbling headfirst into more trouble with my abuser if they confronted her. Once it settled in as a fact that no one was going to believe me, I began to worry the beating would be worse if they had believed me because someone would confront her. Then she would have confronted me but worse. My mind wound in a circle of torture. This non-support system consisted of two or three teachers, the caseworker, and the principal.

Finally, I got tied up and received blow after blow, leaving bruises everywhere that couldn't be explained away, and lived to tell. This was in seventh grade, and good friends warned me that they were going to the teachers if I did not. So, I took my first shower in many years at the school, not having had to since I was homeless. I stood at the sink, staring blankly in the mirror. I washed off the makeup and stormed into a counselor's office. When the caseworker showed up and found out that I had been telling the truth for seven full-blown years, she crumbled and literally left her job. She had been an investigator. Her main job was to pull abused children out of heinous situations. Before reworking her own life, that same "investigator" came back in the office to take pictures of my face without makeup. She believed me then. I had no clothes other than what stuck to me like patches of misfit swatches. There was even one instance, after being told I was lying three times, where I worried for days. I couldn't sleep several nights in a row, and in delirium, I even began to think perhaps I was making the stories up. And if I was, boy…were these stories colorful!

When I was removed from Connie's home, the case worker found hundreds of pills for a diagnosis of bipolar disorder in my toybox because I didn't want to take anything from Connie's hand into my mouth. Everything she touched was poisonous to me. Because of her lies, I was diagnosed with certain conditions, and she told the therapist regularly that I was doing so much better on the meds;

she had no idea I had not been taking the pills. I was not properly diagnosed. Connie, and because of her stories, my therapists, always wanted to control my behavior or state of mind to cover up the rampant abuse. I was not a troubled child. I was an abused child. This is an important distinction. So many victims of abuse are convolutedly made to feel or even believe *they* are the "troublemaker" and given medicine to "correct" them. It's as if society refuses to see the magnitude of evil that human beings are capable of; to do so would demand too much action, too much change, so we lazily allow oppression in all forms to fester and boil over.

Connie was charged with a low-level account of battery after seven years of inflicting physical pain. Every time I told an authority figure, the one thing the school system caseworker did right was take pictures. There was never a charge brought up or follow-up. Always days and weeks of fear, anxiety, and depression. Never help. Still, pictures dating back from the first grade, with bruises all over my face, created the collage of abuse all the way through the seventh grade. I would be beat on Sundays and then miss school on Mondays. All the documentation exists. I would wash my shirts and hang them in the teacher's lounge to dry. My situation wasn't documented in a "foster care" system. Remember: I was sold to Connie as my "legal guardian" and not placed into actual foster care until a new caseworker took over after this fifth account of abuse that I had mustered up the courage to inform the principal. Seven years of abuse. My ability to trust adults, and people, was deeply fragmented.

Years later, right after graduation, I wrote a letter to the principal when I turned nineteen. My words were sincere: "Every punch I took was a result of your negligence of not believing survivors." I meant that I suffered the blows, in part, because of her culpability, lack of compassion, and utter blindness to the very population (the most vulnerable, at that) she oversaw. I ended my message by letting her know after all these years, I had forgiven her. And that I hoped her current and future school staff would foster open discussions about adults believing children and open investigations, even when it's not the easy choice.

I wasn't the only abused kid in that classroom, I'm sure. It seems that the adults refused to believe us. Was that because the school would lose funding? Was it because they weren't equipped with competent social workers to deal with these issues and couldn't call someone? Was their disregard a form of reputational damage control? Or was it that in all honesty, they did not care about kids' welfare if their paychecks were intact?

CHAPTER 6
Luxury and Misery

"Don't tell me the moon is shining; show
me the glint of light on broken glass."

—*Anton Chekhov, playwright*

I WOULD ALWAYS conceal that I was a foster kid. This information conveyed no positive connotations for me, so I would avoid telling anyone about the group and foster homes I had been forced to shuffle in and out of. I thought it would be perceived as a rather significant gap or weakness in my life, and more importantly, I still cringe at the thought of being pitied. I wanted at least to be judged for how I overcame childhood trauma, not for the adversity itself, which was out of my control.

Before I jump into this moment of luxury, I want to acknowledge my white privilege. As hard of a life as I had, it was not made harder because of the color of my skin. As I think about abuse victims in areas like where I grew up, a predominately white rural area with fewer parents and children of color, I am even more fearful of the culture that abused children are not believed. Had I not been white, I believe I would likely not have been given the chance to be heard and believed. Where would I be now? This is important for me to share because our various identities (for me, being gay and for others, being a child of color) have an impact on who may believe us, who may adopt or foster us, and who may abuse us. Statistically, the probability of surviving—let alone, thriving—after childhood trauma is still significantly lower for children of color.

In the first foster home that opened its doors after I practically leaped out of Connie's house onto the hip of a silent but efficient caseworker, there were different rules, separating me, the "foster kid," from their adopted children. My clothes, which were always two sizes too big, were purchased for me at Goodwill, whereas the adopted kids were able to go shopping for almost anything they wanted. After about six months, I had convinced my caseworker to find me a new home, which turned out to be more like a mansion compared to previous homes.

When the day came that I got placed into a luxurious foster home at thirteen, I thought I was dreaming, not because my environs were so plush with a pool and games, but because they had converted the garage into my very own bedroom, a first in nine years. They gave me my first cell phone, which made me feel like I had some degree of independence. This home environment and stability boosted my opportunities and started to shape my identity more positively. That was the dream. I served as captain of show choir, which won numerous awards. I soared every day, even while ensnared in the "normal" turbulence that most seventh graders endure during middle school. My foster mom loved hearing me sing—so much that she would buy me new computer games in exchange for singing. She supported me in everything I wanted to pursue. She even drove me hours away to attend talent shows. Finally, someone at home was proud of me. They made me feel wanted. The music was back, too.

Every year, only the best vocalist students were chosen for a weekend jubilee performed by Jordan Jazz, and Bobby McFerrin (of "Don't Worry, Be Happy" fame) was a guest teacher when I scored a spot. Choir director Judy Hubbard saw the light in me early on and helped me shine. Mrs. Hubbard ended up being one of my biggest supporters throughout middle and high school. All six years, she protected me and was the first person in my life who showed me "tough love" in every aspect of life, not just singing. She pushed me to practice every day. She diligently monitored my academics and made sure I wasn't getting into trouble. She drove me to our competitions, and I was her assistant during sixth period in which she'd let me use the time to help prepare music for the other students or study for a difficult test. I finally had consistency in my life.

My foster parents would drive me an hour to go to the mall or to the movies. I don't remember seeing clothes with tags on them until this family bought me an entire wardrobe. We would all cook together. I was seldom told "no" for anything reasonable I asked for…until they found out that I was gay.

The one family I finally felt some connection with gave me the ultimatum around the ninth grade: either "be straight" like the other foster brothers and their biological son or move out of their home. Despite this big security blanket—and it was rather cozy—I remained defiant. I finally had built up some self-confidence. I was not going to remain in a home trying to convert me into being someone I knew I was not. I had to be myself. Even if it once again evoked feelings of being unwanted, to deny myself would be to un-accept, un-want, unlove myself. There were no open foster homes (and certainly none that would take in an LGBTQ person) in New Castle, so I was forced into the group home, a fancy name for the orphanage in the county.

In the blink of an eye, I was placed in an orphanage with dozens of kids sleeping in a cold dorm. As I entered the room, panic filled my lungs. Captivity. I had been freed to experience fresh air, environs, opportunities, then flung into another kind of confinement. All I could see was bunk bed after bunk bed, maybe twenty. Each flimsy bed the "home" of a child.

Some of these children turned out to be thieves and violent juvenile criminals. I didn't have a winter coat since I couldn't take any of the clothes with me from my previous homophobic house. Without protection by employees, I was bullied because of my lisp, which is still somehow associated with being gay. Now, at age fourteen, lisp or not, I figured a few kids would like me and that would be enough to get by in this cold place. Cookie-cutter schedules and responsibilities ruled the orphanage, with having to go to lunch at the same time, "study" and sleep in tandem with scores of people. Lying on my tiny island of a bed with eighteen to twenty other kids surrounding me, I thought of my brutal and dark journey. I didn't cry, didn't freeze in helplessness. At least no one was "pretending" to love me here. I didn't have to maintain a coverup—makeup or mask. Being amongst one of many, I could effortlessly blend into the crowd (when I didn't speak with a lisp). These circumstances felt less traumatic than being forced to abandon my identity. I would never again have to pretend to be someone's version of what is considered "wanted."

I still thought of my mother often, as I grew to understand that she couldn't regain custody. I knew I wouldn't see her again. I hadn't since I was seven years old. The state stopped looking for her after a couple of years, anyway, stating that this was in my best interest—that being in Connie's home was in my best interest, then tossed around. Because the state never terminated my mother's rights though, I could only be fostered, never adopted.

It's worth noting that one of the major advantages of adoption is increased stability for the child. If a child has been living with their foster family for months or years before they become eligible for adoption (meaning, they likely have no origin home or biological and *fit* parents to return to), they have presumably formed attachments to their foster parents, siblings, home, school, and community. Being adopted allows them to maintain relationships that are important to them and prevents them from having to move and start over with a new family. But I remained ineligible for adoption because my mother still had an open door to seek custody again one day. In fact, I remember a few times when my friends' families would offer to take me in, only to be rejected due to the arduous, tangled process that adoption entails.

With my mother gone, I had to make the most of my life through optimizing the scholarships and insurance payments from my late father that I was eligible for as an "orphan." I had to traverse this captivity first, these teenage scavengers wanting to fight, watching my every move, eyes glowing in the dark when "lights out" time came.

CHAPTER 7

Trust—It's Complicated

"Trust is like blood pressure. It's silent, vital to
good health, and if abused it can be deadly."

—*FRANK SONNENBERG, AUTHOR AND ADVOCATE*

As a sophomore in high school, I finally had close friends and even
cultivated a support system. But I still didn't trust many adults.
Every adult that knew of my pain and scarcity either inflicted it or
didn't do anything about it.

Assessing trust in intimate relationships and the self-perception
process for *The Journal of Social Psychology*, multiple doctor-authors
agree: "Trust is the act of placing confidence in someone or something else. It is a fundamental human experience. Trust is necessary
for society to function. It can play a significant role in happiness.
Without it, fear rules. Some life experiences can impact a person's
ability to trust others."

The piece goes on to describe scenarios that result in trust issues:
a lack of care and acceptance or being mistreated as children, social

rejection in one's teens, or being betrayed or belittled during the formative years. Each impacts self-esteem. I experienced them all.

For me, I had an inherent desire to trust people, and I still do. I was not naturally skeptical, cynical, or bitter. Amazingly, I avoided becoming all these things. I had hope, no matter how dim it may have become at different points of my life. I never permitted my negative experiences to burn out my candle. I just did not have any examples of model adults to trust.

Then I met Beth.

When I met Beth, I trusted her in the first hour of our time together. Beth, whose one of many specialties was monitoring and advocating for children on course for independent living, became my caseworker. This trust was a new feeling of psychological safety, and not because she always called me "a special young man!" Beth had lived in New Castle, my hometown, her whole life. She had a B.S. in English literature from Indiana University, yet she had been working for child services since 1986. I was attracted to her range of knowledge and her warm personality. I could tell she loved her job and the children and families she met. Sometimes I wanted to spend more time with her, but I knew how rampantly understaffed and overworked caseworkers are; regardless, she would always keep a close eye on me, balancing the need for mutual trust with making sure all her foster kids were safe.

Beth was always skilled at pushing limits and trying new things to fulfill my needs. In fact, she often put her career at risk going out on a limb for me. As our bond strengthened, she introduced me to a new family—her very own, with warm invites to their Thanksgiving celebrations where I was treated not like a foster kid but one of her sons. While the treasure of feeling loved was still foreign, she made it a household name in my heart.

Beth may have not known it at the time, but she inspired me to be my true self. She accepted me as an orphan. As gay. She showed me how to love myself, and that is one of the greatest gifts I could have ever received—it was the first step in possessing the strength to love others, truly. Beth is arguably the reason I recovered after hearing bad news, fought for first place in music competitions, strove for an "A" on a test, got admitted into college, and accepted others for who they are. Beth supported me as I even learned to trust myself more deeply. Sometimes the feeling of worthiness will change your entire attitude on life. She gave me the gift of feeling worthy.

My sophomore year, Beth placed me with new foster parents: "Joseph" and "Sheila." They are models of what and why good, hard-working people (ones truly in it for the children and not themselves or the money) become foster parents.

They were the first foster parents in my life who told me they would love me, regardless of whom I loved. Was our relationship perfect? Not at all! I do separate my experience under their guardianship, which was positive overall, from that of others in my life since the day I left my mother's truck to the time I entered independent living. They were the only guardians, true court-appointed guardians, in my life I was able to build real and authentic relationships with.

Joseph and Sheila decided they wouldn't have kids of their own early in their relationship. They knew that they wanted to adopt or foster, as Joseph put it, "as there are plenty of children in the world but not enough parents." They were special, working with a specific organization that served as a home to help children after they had participated in an assessment program to determine if they could be placed into a more permanent foster care situation. They worked with children who were on probation, some with social disabilities, or suffered any number of other challenging situations or problems. The foster program and county knew that Sheila and Joseph had the heart to take nearly any child offered, even if they had been turned down by others.

The organization itself was a religiously affiliated one, and while that can be a problem for gay children, Joseph and Sheila never allowed it to be for me. As devout Quakers, one belief in the religion is that everyone possesses a *personal* relationship with God. With their guidance and through their accepting nature that I, too, was able to finally rectify my relationship with my God and who I was deep down. I never believed in fate, but always wondered: *Why me? What had I done?* But the thought of having a "higher power" who allowed or forced me to endure what I faced just never seemed to make sense to me.

Beth called and pleaded for them to take me out of the wretched orphanage. Because of my history with the county foster program for years, I did not need the initial assessment to be placed with Joseph and Sheila. I also had the opportunity to get acquainted with their godson through choir and school activities. Most importantly, they took me in knowing I had been removed from the previous home. I had a hunch Joseph knew that they discarded me for being gay.

Joseph and Sheila supported me in all my involvement as a social and academically active kid, going so far as to drive me to a school further away than where their other kids went so that I could stay in the school that I had grown to love and with the tribe I finally integrated with. The opportunities (choir, speech, and debate, etc.) in the city school were more ample than the area we lived in, and they saw me thrive. They gave me the gift of stability. I remember thinking at last, the "system" was starting to work for me.

Joseph taught me to drive a manual transmission over the course of frustrating evenings in the school parking lot trying to take off and shift gears. I sure could get frustrated, but I desperately wanted that car for unbridled independence.

Joseph thought enough of my passion for music to drive me to see "Rent" in Indianapolis, the big city (to me)! We were both mesmerized. Even though I had not disclosed that I was gay, I was comfortable enough to watch the incredible story with my new foster parents about the struggles of LGBTQ people living with HIV in New York.

Despite our meaningful engagement, the ability to trust them took significantly longer to develop. When I lived with Joseph and Sheila, life still felt chaotic. They were saints for taking on challenging foster kids, but with the way they rotated in and out of the home, fear of trust gripped me because I couldn't trust the other kids that they parented alongside me. They encouraged me to be friends with the other boys, but several of them bullied me at school—one to the point of threatening to taser me. This wasn't Joseph and Sheila's fault.

For roughly two years, they did all they could to create some sense of normalcy in the house. I understand that desire as guardians trying to maintain a healthy environment, else the whole house of cards crumbles. In the grand scheme of things, because of my age and identity that I cemented in that cold orphanage every night when the lights went out, I was probably too rebellious in their eyes, needlessly disrupting the peace sometimes. But perhaps that's why I am who I am today, and brave enough to write and share my story.

In hindsight, I know they saw so much potential in me, which is paramount during an adolescent's development. An adult's validation and encouragement morphs into pride for the child. I just didn't have the mental capacity to recognize it.

Although this may be a bit selfish and was not my most mature viewpoint, I was always embarrassed to be seen in the home and even with them because of the association to all the baggage of what other kids had done regardless of how well-behaved I had been through everything. I fought my whole life for people to *not* see me as homeless. Not abused. Not an orphan. Right or wrong, I was socialized to worry about others' perceptions of me in my desperate quest for acceptance. For my own sense of normalcy.

I was also harder on Sheila than I needed to be. Foster children, especially boys, regularly have more challenging relationships with the foster mom for many reasons. I had a storied history with women, to say the least. Sheila was doing her best to raise me and instill in me discipline I never had to clean the room, sit at the dinner table with the "family" on time, be responsible. Without question, she tried hard to establish trust between us. However, my next set of moves mangled it, and in the process of writing this book and interviewing them for my story, I discovered that I had ultimately hurt them when it was time for me to live independently.

At this point, I still had a lot of work to do on myself. The system was forcing me to spend so much of my time in therapy on the events of the day that I couldn't work on myself and my past. So, when I hit age sixteen, it got to the point where I aimed to live independently as soon as possible, freeing myself from the burden of everyone else's labels on my identity.

Beth fully supported me, trusted me, and fought for me to transition out of the foster care system. However, Joseph and Sheila did not want me to leave their family unit. Sheila wrote a letter to my counselor emphasizing that they always cared about me and wanted the best for me.

Looking back, I know that withholding the pursuit of my dream for emancipation and going behind their backs to be on my own hurt them (Sheila especially). She took some of the rationale I filed with the court hard and more personally than I ever meant.

In a letter to my school counselor, Sheila wrote:

> I will always care about you and want
> wonderful things for you. I want you to have
> all the material things that are so important to
> you. I want you to have good friends and good
> health. I want you to be successful and have
> the brilliant career in law you always wanted.
> More importantly, I want you to realize the
> importance of people, not things. I want you
> to choose friends because of the type people
> they are and not because of what they look like,

how much money they have, or what they can do for you. Build your relationships on rock, not sand. I also want you to learn to respect and love yourself, which is something I don't believe you have ever truly done. Youth and beauty are ephemeral; intelligence, respect for truth, caring, generosity, a good reputation, a solid value system, and empathy for others are true measures of a person's worth.

Socrates said, "The unexamined life is not worth living." It has been one of my favorite quotes and I think it is a great truth. He also said, "Think not those faithful who praise all thy words and actions; but those who kindly reprove your faults."

I regret any pain I caused them. My quest for independence, growth toward forgiveness and self-love, and wanting to be accepted by friends at school all drove me beyond my need to participate in this household. No matter how much they included me, I still felt on my own. Joseph and Sheila may never know the profound and positive impact they had on me. It helps to reflect on it now.

CHAPTER 8

Hard Work and Hard-Earned Independence

> "Promise me you will always remember—
> you are braver than you believe, stronger than
> you seem, and smarter than you think.
>
> -CHRISTOPHER ROBIN, FROM "WINNIE THE POOH"

IT STARTED WHEN I was ten. I dreamed of the day of being independent. During what may have been my third year living with Connie, facing emotional abuse daily and physical abuse on average three to four times a week, I knew I'd be better off alone. I'm so fortunate that I desired to be by myself, as so many kids in the foster care system and many more in cycles of abuse would perhaps conceive of worse. To me, at least being alone meant I had more control of my own destiny and experience.

This desire only picked up steam being cast from home to home. *Emancipation*, a legal term used for those orphans and children who are "freed" from the foster care system gave me important agency, or purpose and some sense of internal power to figure that out. I never wanted to be associated with anyone or anything against my will again.

But there was a way out: while I could not be legally emancipated due to existing parental rights, "independent living" was the next best thing. I longed to create my own environments, my own home, my own friendships, my own family. It was also a journey to prove myself. To trust myself. In the end, it was one of the best things I could have ever done for myself.

When the judge gave her ruling—that I could live on my own—I felt free! I could release the persistent fear that a foster parent could shove me back in an orphanage for any reason they chose. No more inhospitable buildings passed off as a home. No more extreme vulnerability and fear that gave me high blood pressure and abnormal heartbeat. (I still take medication for this, but at least I can control the stressors that may contribute.) This special Independence Day was a holiday I will never forget.

I had learned to be quite persuasive. Throughout my time living with Joseph and Sheila, on top of all my school and extracurriculars, I always worked. I started working when I was fifteen at McDonalds, taking a lot of persuasion to get them to hire me. I worked nearly every day after school, show choir, or speech and debate. I needed the money, and a work schedule continued teaching me discipline I had never had in my life.

Then I graduated to Wendy's and smelled like a junior bacon burger 24/7. From circle burgers to square biscuits, I cooked, packaged, and served customers with a big smile! But something about the new, fancy Starbucks in New Castle beckoned me. Many days, I would leave work and walk to the store to ask about open positions. I was young, but I could see the more positive work environment, attitude, and impact their corporate culture had on their employees. I wanted, like Starbucks, to be in the people business happening to sell coffee. Inevitably, I befriended the store manager and after weeks, maybe months, of persuasion, she offered a job.

Over the next three years in high school, I worked at Starbucks and became a star barista. I befriended customers, and the other baristas always wanted to work my shift because, well, I am a fun guy (at least I keep myself amused to this day!). I was the first person that some customers saw before they had their first cup of coffee, an opportunity that I seized every morning to help others' day begin on a high note. I delivered all the sunshine I could. One woman, face blotched with tears, told me she was going through a divorce. I could feel her anguish, so I took a break and had a cup of coffee with her.

This dedication to hard work, good grades, and meaningful engagement with others contributed to succeeding in my goal of living independently.

The furniture and decorations in my first house were, well, bare. I didn't have family trinkets or photos from family vacations to display. But I earned enough money for a computer for school, dial-up Internet, and necessities. On top of it all, I was more determined than ever to have a solid education. Somehow through all this, I always prioritized my academics. Once I got approved for independent living, thanks to Beth, a slew of doors swung open to me. As a junior, I wrote an essay that got me accepted into a prestigious week-long leadership summit and mock trial for aspiring attorneys. Most importantly, I came out to my entire high school. It wasn't a ceremonial occasion like dancing and singing it through the halls, sun cascading against the lockers as everyone clapped. It was more like a trickle effect of short conversations with various groups.

Beth's take on that big move reflects what a lot of gay kids have gone through. Of course, previous generations of LGBTQ+ people had it harder than I did, and I am thankful for their struggles, sacrifices, and contributions.

Beth said, "I was scared that it would not go well. New Castle is a small Midwestern town with many small Midwestern minds. Mat was so well-liked that he suffered no repercussions, except one teacher who just told him, 'No, you are not gay!'"

Beth is speaking of my choir teacher, who arguably made me a star. I know she didn't say that as a bad thing; I think it was from a place of heart—not wanting me to suffer. Either way, both women saw me flourish, and I sincerely thank them for the deep impressions they made on my life.

Senior Honor Day was such a mixed set of emotions. I remember it vividly. I was awarded various honors and thirteen different scholarships, from local community groups and a few from talent competitions, for singing. I was astonished. Prouder than I had ever been. I smiled. I cried. I smiled again. Cried. A bright future summoned me. Beth was there carrying the torch of pride for me.

My industrious spirit still drove me. Rather than go out to party with friends, I worked at Starbucks and closed the store that night. Then on my graduation day a few weeks later, I opened the store after having the opportunity to give a speech to my high school student government. I remember telling my classmates to embrace themselves for who they are—something that I learned from Sheila. As one of the few out, gay people in rural Indiana, I was chosen for another term.

I wish all case workers could be more like Beth. She worked vigorously on behalf of others and freely showed her compassion and empathy. Sometimes in dark and dismal territory, I'm sure, knowing what I experienced in rural Indiana.

In a blatant display of favoritism, in my senior year, Beth wanted to throw me a graduation party, but upon asking her superiors, she learned that doing so would be a conflict of interest. Another weird state law. A conflict of interest to throw one of the kids, alone and under your oversight, a graduation party to celebrate this high school achievement? Well, that did not stop Beth. She risked her career so she could host a celebration for me.

CHAPTER 9
Forgiveness is the Lantern

"Forgiveness is not always easy. At times, it
feels more painful than the wound we suffered,
to forgive the one that inflicted it. And yet,
there is no peace without forgiveness."

-MARIANNE WILLIAMSON, SPIRITUAL LEADER

LANTERN FESTIVAL, ALSO called Yuan Xiao Festival, is a holiday celebrated in China and other Asian countries honoring deceased ancestors on the 15th day of the first month (Yuan) of the lunar calendar. The Lantern Festival aims to promote reconciliation, peace, and forgiveness. A legend concerning the festival's origin tells the tale of the Jade Emperor (You Di), who became angered at a town for killing his goose. He planned to destroy the town with fire, but he was thwarted by a fairy who advised the people to light lanterns across the town on the appointed day of destruction. The emperor, fooled by all the light, assumed the town was already engulfed in flames. The town was spared, and in gratitude, the people continued to commemorate the event annually by carrying colorful lanterns throughout the town.

Atlanta hosts its own version every year, and this nighttime wonderland has made me think about forgiveness a lot.

Forgiveness is a potpourri of self-awareness, inquiry, maturity, and empathy. Through all the happiness of my high school years, in my newfound independence and freedom, I still had immense drama from my past. The hardest part of my life was recognizing how toxic these things were and obsessing about nearly every thought. I'd been fortunate to undergo therapy for several years at this point, and the few times the therapist broached the idea of how I felt about those people in my past and if I could forgive them, the answer was no. Often a belligerent, rageful no. How could I ever forgive?

Then I realized that forgiveness is legitimately about *you*. It is an important, one of the most important, steps out of the dark. It became, for me, a lantern lighting the way to my own ability to move past all the dark times. It took me many years to reconcile that I had done nothing wrong, nothing to deserve the pain and neglect. Forgiveness is empowering. Liberating. And very productive. Bishop TD Jakes said, "I think the first step is to understand that forgiveness does not exonerate the perpetrator. Forgiveness liberates the victim. It's a gift you give yourself."

The thorns in my side from my past were still ever present and not in the distant past. When I graduated from high school, I found out Connie, my abuser, and my "real" father, Charlie—the one who gave me the bike—were now dating. Just out of the blue. Dating. It was a disturbing announcement that took me back, what seemed like years, to a place of severe pain. The man who was supposedly my biological father that never parented me and the brutal guardian who feigned being my parent and abused me physically and emotionally for seven years—*together*.

At first, it was almost too much to bear. But then I held onto the joys of how far I had walked since climbing out of the back of that pickup truck at the age of six, all that I had accomplished on my own and come to terms with. Now that I trusted people, I felt free. I felt the need to forgive.

At the age of seventeen, I drove Joseph and Sheila's car to visit Charlie's house where I told Connie in person that I forgave her for years of physical and emotional abuse. She started sobbing. She had no explanation, no further insults.

After giving myself that gift, I was on my way to finding real success, in life and love. Although I hadn't begun to fully comprehend it at first, I was liberated from the Indiana foster care system. It's a system that I didn't willingly enter, but I sure as hell exited with elation.

CHAPTER 10
Pride and Persuasion

"Freedom is the oxygen of the soul."

—MOSHE DAYAN, MILITARY LEADER

THIS SKILL OF mine made a roaring impact on my life when it was time to go to college. Many people in my life have claimed that I possess a persuasive nature. I may be persuasive, but it was never for malicious intent growing up. I wanted to live a secure place in the world and to secure my own reality. I craved belonging, love, acceptance. Being wanted. I'm not sure if my persuasiveness is a natural gift or something I developed on my path, but it has helped me on my quest to a safer, brighter future. It helped me get my first job at McDonald's before I was supposed be old enough to work; it helped me secure my own emancipation from the state. I wasn't afraid to try to convince a few high school teachers for the occasional extra time for assignments to keep up my grades. I talked my way out of situations that intuitively felt negative or nonproductive. I set my sights on something and planned; then I worked diligently to obtain it. To quote another excerpt of Sheila's letter to my counselor, she said, "Intelligence is not just making good grades (which Mat did). It is also being able to decide what you want, figure all the angles and possibilities, and find a way to go after it."

Throughout high school, Beth wisely kept hinting that I should go to a public university where I would have received a full ride. While she would often give me advice, she was the first person to understand that I did not need a "parent" to be happy. She was more like a favorite aunt—she looked after me as closely as she could, but she gave me the respect of letting me be a young man, allowing me the freedom to ultimately make my own decisions.

I was hellbent on going to my dream private school, Butler University in Indianapolis. This desire was all due to my love of music, my one saving grace in school—the place I first had an adult truly take interest in me.

Butler is internationally renowned for jazz studies, dance, and music production, but I had a scholarship from the state that could only be used for attendance at a state college. I legitimately found and applied for every scholarship (large or small) I might be eligible for. In the end, at the age of eighteen, I was the first freshman to get selected for the Jordan Jazz vocal group, a small ensemble of twelve student jazz singers studying in Butler University's School of Music. Up until now, music had always been a driving force, lighting the path to a brighter future for me.

I chose that path. I charged into Butler solely on sheer determination and adrenaline. Translation: I didn't have a dime! And not only as a first-generation college student, but I was also honestly the only generation in my family in some ways…I did not fully understand what I was getting myself into. Those jobs that kept me afloat in high school, Starbucks and McDonalds, were little help with affording a private school. But I had music. And I made friends.

On top of Jordan Jazz, I was one of about thirty freshmen accepted into Butler's Ambassadors of Change program (AOC), a week-long leadership conference where I met my first, true best friend. I was well-liked by many in high school, but I never felt like I had a friend who understood me. During the program, we learned from the juniors and seniors how to instill leadership in our future classmates. Then came Marisa who was such an inspiration—she lived a small Midwestern life like me, and she shared my determination to overcome this in early adulthood. She even inspired me to run for class president (I lost to a basketball star). In fact, Marisa was elected class vice president and became a model leader for the school; thirteen years later, she's still a model leader in her community.

In one of my freshman classes, I quickly befriended one of the brightest, fiercest women I had ever met, also named Marissa (with two S's). Marissa was among my most influential peers at school, as she seemingly aced every class, regularly while even having to tutor me, given that we tried to take every class together. Despite her living in the girls' dorm, Marissa and I were inseparable, sharing all the exciting new college experiences together, giving honest counsel to each other on every topic on almost everything personal. She would ensure I had somewhere to spend college breaks when the dorms were closed, effectively making me homeless again each time. Her parents took me in, also treating me as a son. Our friendship was based on the safe space we created for one another based on the foundation of trust. I *finally* had two peers with whom I could be honest in every aspect of my life. She and Marisa became my chosen family.

Once I got settled into dorm life (kind of a joke in my eyes, as it was like a hedonistic paradise for rich, straight kids and refined compared to most of my own digs growing up), I realized I didn't have money for the basics since by this time, I had spent it on literally everything tied to my education. I couldn't eat or drink books and musical instruments.

I broke down and called Joseph and Sheila, who drove to Butler and gave me some spending money and toiletries, with well wishes. This is what it feels like to be loved unconditionally! Even through the pain we shared, they still were there for me in a dark moment.

Fortunately, it wasn't just my own persuasion lighting my path. Serendipitously, I had a new mentor in Don Young, who had obtained his master's degree at Butler. He was a highly empathetic, patient, and smart speech pathologist, who had chosen me to become a mentor for his students when I was still in high school; being a mentor was of my favorite community service activities. He also happened to be gay, so I sought his counsel about dorm life.

As we grew closer, Don, whom I began viewing more like an uncle, offered to rent his spare room to me for the summer, given that school housing was not offered. A lot of college kids fight homelessness in the summer, and often go hungry like I did. Don was a godsend mentor to me because in no time, living on campus, all at once, I went through what normal people do in their late teens and early twenties over the period of decades. I never had the chance to rebel in high school; I was always an adult. I didn't drink, despite having an entire house to myself during senior year of high school. I didn't get into trouble. I didn't have that luxury since life was already fragile enough starting as a six-year-old with adult responsibilities.

As many college freshmen do, I took up drinking…a lot. I had too many years of experimentation to get out of my system. Of course, addiction is often genetic; however, while I knew this, I still often turned to alcohol to quell my anxiety and depression before I could afford healthcare to see a doctor about managing these mental health challenges. Uncle Don was always a positive role model, and he understood my trauma, given that he spent his career helping kids who had experienced similar situations. He went so far as buying a car from his brother, which he loaned me until I could afford my own.

During this time with Don, I learned how amazing Cher is (his idol), how to socialize better, listen, and operate my life from a place of newness and curiosity rather than based on the fragmentations and shards of the past.

Don was also the first adult to discuss politics and views with me. At first, I didn't have a political affiliation but not because I didn't care about political issues. I cared, but it took a lot of time and energy to manage the PTSD! Between the actual abuse itself, stepping in and out of places called "home," staring down repercussions of unintended yet still activated reactions from the negative events, and studying to mold an identity based on achievement rather than said traumas, there isn't much room or time in a young adult's mind to form convictions. This is far from the person I am today, as you will soon learn. But I think it's important to note because foster kids can get a bad rap for seemingly "not caring" about anything, like work or school. Often the trauma we experience in those settings hinder own ability to form meaningful convictions and concerns.

College was a blast. In between the frat parties and Friday night bar crawls, I was in heaven singing for one of the top college groups in the world. The audition the summer before school started required me to walk in the door, pick up a piece of music and sing it (sight-read) on the spot in front of everyone. I also had to sing a prepared song. Mrs. Hubbard, my vocal teacher since sixth grade and one of the first people to believe in me, drove me to the audition and accompanied me on the piano.

I sang the song "Raindrops Will Fall" by Tamyra Gray. The lyrics perfectly encompassed where I was in life.

I walked through the fire, oh
Fought through the ragin' storm
Till I found the peace that's inside of me
I've got to be strong
I stand for my dreams
I was made for this moment

From there, college life blossomed. Soon, I took my first flight to go on a weeks-long jazz tour in Asia, and it wasn't easy. Yes, my first flight ever was a fifteen-hour trip to Hong Kong…and I was an anxious, hyper kid. No one had briefed me on flying or given me any tips for international travel. Those original iPods did not hold a charge long enough to make it across the Canadian shield, as the plane made its way from New York over the North Pole. Oh, the turbulence! I'm quite sure, ironically enough, this was one of the first times in my life, even after all I had been through, where I truly wasn't sure if I would make it out alive on the other side.

Still, I made it to Hong Kong in one piece. We worked with early elementary schools, inspiring kids there to learn vocal jazz and even helped implement vocal jazz studies in multiple universities in a part of the globe where the sounds were completely different. The teachers praised us. I confided in them that all I wanted was to perform on Broadway, despite my limited vocal range.

Butler was one of the most exciting times in my life, but at the conclusion of three successful semesters, Butler shut the door in my face near the end of third semester, which put me $20,000 in debt, and they withheld my transcripts so I couldn't transfer. They marked my education "unpaid" because most of my loans were never approved since I had no co-signer in 2009, during the height of the financial crisis. What is strange is that Butler never notified me of this until after fifteen weeks of the semester had gone by.

I stormed into the dean's office, finance office, and even the president's mansion in tears asking for help. Financial aid is confusing enough to people who have folks who can help them. At this point, no one in the administration would help me either. I still feel a stab of pain over this. Apparently, I had talked and sung my way into an expensive program that needed to be paid for in cash since I had no one to co-sign loans with me. Perhaps not the most practical decision I had ever made, but who can blame an eighteen-year-old who had been deprived of so many other things in life?

I couldn't pursue music or academics thereafter because now, I wasn't tied to any organizations or schools. Butler would not allow me to obtain my transcripts required to transfer until I paid thousands back directly to the university. My account was sent to collections, killing my credit score, hindering my ability to take on the minimum of credit card debt until I could find a job. Even after a year of finally feeling accepted, being proud of my accomplishments as a vocalist, a chance for this orphan to travel the world, I was left alone. Defeated. And it created an awful cycle. I needed a job to pay this bill, could not get back into school until it was paid, and my heart yearned to complete this special music education, the dream that helped me survive my childhood.

I spent days, even weeks, trying to find a job that paid more than minimum wage. I then landed a job with a Delta affiliate processing flights as a gate agent, and with it came flight benefits. In some ways, this was a lucky step in my journey. I was thrilled to see a whole globe outside of rural Indiana. The world busted open its doors and nourished me mentally, emotionally, and spiritually. I welcomed every place that I could steal memories from. I befriended locals I met at bars and coffee shops. In no time, it felt like I was traveling more than I worked, though I was finally able to pay Butler enough for them to release my transcripts.

The end of summer was fast approaching. Something inside me rang an alarm bell: *Return to school.*

As much as I loved this airline industry job, and as much as I loved my crazy weekends in cities all over the country, I knew that

I had to get back to work on completing my education. Although it was not the "fun" choice to leave my flight benefits behind, it wouldn't pay the bank of my life in the end. With the decision to return to school, bigger plans ensued.

CHAPTER 11

Resisting the Cocktail of Dysfunction

"Addiction, at its worst, is akin to having Stockholm
Syndrome. You're like a hostage who has developed
an irrational affection for your captor. They can
abuse you, torture you, even threaten to kill you, and
you'll remain inexplicably and disturbingly loyal."

—*Anne Clendening, singer*

Without any experience in the field of law, a paralegal position
opened to me. I had a demonstrated, impressive work ethic, but I
could hardly believe it! A friend from my management class told me
she would put in a good word, and I got hired on the spot. I didn't
do any vetting of the company because I needed the money to continue paying off my debt from Butler to obtain my transcripts and
apply for admittance elsewhere. And boy, it paid a lot better than
some of my previous jobs.

It was always a life goal for me to obtain a college degree, and even though I was so young, I felt like time would run out on me before I could achieve this goal. Sadly, kids today, especially those who have no family or resources, are forced to incur a mountain of student debt to measure their lives' worthiness, a cycle of inequity that has continued to grow exorbitantly over decades. I was lucky to find someone to hire me for a better-paying job who valued my grit and tenacity over a college diploma.

I worked at the law firm for more than three years, fifty hours a week. On top of this, although I had been studying business at Butler (pre-law), I was accepted into the Indiana University School for Public and Environmental Affairs, an internationally ranked program that educates students on policy, business, and global affairs at their IUPUI campus, a satellite campus in Indianapolis.

Throughout my life, learning to advocate for *myself* gave me the determination that I wanted to do something that would make a difference in the world for *other people.* As fate would have it, perhaps I needed the hard lesson from Butler to get me into a program that allowed me greater opportunity to chart career paths to make a difference in the world than my studies at Butler would have afforded me.

My new overzealous boss, who almost commanded a seat on an important court that year, took a chance on me in my early twenties and paved the way for my success today. We had a peculiar relationship, however. She never had children of her own, so she often treated me as a "son." Although it would have been nice (maybe) to have a mother figure as a boss, unfortunately, her occasional motherly ways, coupled with my need for autonomy, strained our relationship.

She hired two administrative people and claimed an entire office all to herself. No exaggeration, I completed all the procurement, contracts, phone, marketing, and web design. I was honored to help the firm create the new law office, but at that time, my interests matured in the law and policy, not taking care of everyday business matters. I later resigned. I will always be enormously grateful for how many lessons that bright woman taught me (and for the shenanigans she put up with in my early twenties).

Within four days, I had another job after an hour-long interview. All in all, things were looking up. But all this work and school did not fill in every hole I had in my existence. Not being able to sing contributed to risky behavior, as this had been the only thing that truly fulfilled me. Emotional scars from decades of abuse and uncertainty manifested in unhealthy ways. I also hit a tough point in my life attempting to balance my hard work with a healthier "party" life.

One night, I was walking home from a pub close to where me and Don lived, having great fun. The problem was that I didn't stop. Finally, I got into a cab and showed the driver my ID so he could take me home. Unfortunately, we had moved two months earlier, so I was driven to the old address on my ID. I was too loaded to realize it, and after trying to open the kitchen window to get inside a place my key obviously didn't work to access, I was so lucky that the occupants recognized me as the previous tenant.

Can you imagine? What a close call, even for a sophomore in college.

The merry-go-round relationship I had with alcohol was a revolving cycle for me throughout my early twenties and even more afterward as I tried hard to cope. After this last incident, I knew I needed to stay away from the bars (at least on weekdays).

Although alcohol did not have an outright material detriment to me, I took myself to Alcoholics Anonymous (AA) meetings on my own, given my family history of addiction. There, I always thought about my mother, wondering if she ever made it to an AA meeting. Was she alive? Homeless again? I'm a Scorpio, and I was born on her birthday, which made my thoughts on the parallel between our personalities even more inescapable.

While you learn many important lessons in AA meetings, the

most valuable lesson for me came from hearing everyone's struggles with addiction, many of whom resulted in ruined relationships, jobs, entire lives. I realized I wasn't addicted; I just needed some sense knocked into me! I remained on track. In my last semester at IU, I took seven classes and got straight "A's." I always had the will for something great. I refused to drown that greatness in the same liquid that wrecked my childhood.

At this point, too, I was alone. My best friends from college, Marissa and Marisa, were in very different places. I was young, and technology started to dominate assorted areas of life. Phone apps and social media started coming in handy for meeting new people. Except for Don and Beth, I felt alone again. The alcohol didn't help.

CHAPTER 12
Chosen Family

"We've all done this—created our mix-and-match families, our homemade safety nets."

—DAVID LEVITHAN, AUTHOR

FAMILY: COMMON GENETICS, ancestral bloodlines, can be one of the best parts of a child's life or the worst. Out there, every type of family imaginable exists. Our society loves to paint a fairy tale picture of what family should be—what your parents should look like, should do, how your childhood and education should evolve, how much love should exist. A whole lot of societal expectations that just, well, break down. I don't need to quote divorce statistics, nor the number of children abandoned and left behind. No one's family relationship is ever 100% ideal.

If you work hard on building close relationships with others, though, if you put out good energy in the world, be a good friend, and open up to people, you can start to develop what some call "chosen" family.

Many LGBTQ people are rejected from their parents and home, then find friends who become like brothers and sisters. Older people in the community like fathers and uncles. I had living relatives, but I didn't know it at the time. I had also begun to construct relationships that finally felt like family. With the advocacy, safety and security Beth afforded me, she became like a chosen mom. Uncle Don, my closest gay mentor, right alongside her. The two of them never missed my call and always had advice. Nevertheless, my peer group was all over the place.

Then I met Zach in 2010. He's my best friend to this day, and the closest relationship I could ever develop to a brother, along with his partner, Jake, like that brother-in-law I love and get along with. Zach's story carries parallels to mine, which cemented our bond quickly. We could talk of our pasts openly and be empathetic to one another even if the stories weren't quite the same.

Over time, we became inseparable. I took on a little more of a big-brother role in many ways. Zach took the role of everything else. A steady rock in my long road of gravel. Zach came from a divided family, having his parents split when he was young, and they were poor. Zach experienced pain early in his life when his brother passed away, further straining the dynamic in his family.

Zach, too, grew up in a family and town rooted in social conservatism, and struggled as a gay kid to find acceptance and love. Zach, too, fought depression. And he too took that risky leap of faith to come out and start living his identity. We had shared trauma painted in unique experiences. What mattered most was our appreciation of each other, our vulnerability together, our shared memories and laughs. Truly chosen family.

No family is perfect. Even chosen ones. I was still struggling with depression and the need for moderation in my life; Zach wanted to escape the situation he'd been in most of his life—small town and narrow minds—but was taking a hiatus from college with little motivation to return to school. Zach had also recently lost his best friend, his brother.

Who knows what brought us together—a higher being, the universe, dumb luck—but we saw so much in each other. Zach recounted when we were talking about this, "What I saw in you, this young man (not even twenty-one) was a brilliant, persevering, resoundingly positive, and insightful soul. Someone my own age, but whose personality and identity made them years wiser. All of this while maintaining the desire to be spontaneous, adventurous, and experience; all the fruits being in your twenties offers you. You didn't just want to wait to experience life, you wanted to *drive* the experience in your life."

Zach and I were each other's main source of encouragement in our early twenties. Zach encouraged me every day to mature, treat life more delicately and less recklessly. It was because we were there as each other's accountability partner (everyone should have one) to make sure we both succeeded. We were both extremely conscientious of each other and tried to build each other up, ensuring neither of us slipped in life.

We were able to coach and help each other with things like going back to college and finding a career path we would be exceptional at. For this book, Zach recalled: "Throughout 2010 and 2011, we became closer and closer. You encouraged me to embrace my identity, to tap into the things I was already good at, and to be tactical in enhancing what I didn't perceive myself to be good at, to enhance myself as a person (i.e., go back to college, think about a real career that both made me happy and proud of my identity). Because of this, I was able to muster up the courage to 'come out' of the closet on all fronts to my family, my co-workers. Embracing my identity was the best feeling I had ever experienced. It was then that we became 'best' friends. Had it not been for meeting you and being empowered with those skills of real empathy and understanding, I would have slipped back into my self-hating depression and wouldn't have been able to be there for you in those times that you needed me as a friend."

This is chosen family.

Writing about the importance of relationships and belonging, Dr. John Sharry, a social worker and psychotherapist and co-developer of the Parents Plus Programmes, points out in *The Irish Times,* "The two major challenges in maintaining close personal relationships are neglect (not putting time into the relationship) and not dealing constructively with conflict (thus, letting problems fester until they are out of control). Being proactive in your personal relationships and attending to them (even when you don't feel like it) is the key to keeping them happy supportive and personally satisfying.

"Relationships are nurtured by frequent displays of appreciation. Whether these are simply kind words of thanks to an important colleague, a gift to an important friend, affection with your partner or a reassuring hug for a child, everyone needs to be appreciated and nurtured in close relationships."

I'm forever indebted to Beth, Don and Zach for our relationship and their impact on my life. I can promise you my chosen family, especially these three who proved their worth to me and loved me for who I am, regardless, is way healthier than a lot of the bloodline relatives out there.

CHAPTER 13
The Wait Is Over

"A deep sense of love and belonging is an irreducible
need of all people. We are biologically, cognitively,
physically, and spiritually wired to love, to be loved,
and to belong. When those needs are not met, we don't
function as we were meant to. We break. We fall apart.
We numb. We ache. We hurt others. We get sick."

—*Brené Brown, research professor and author*

I used to cry endlessly to Zach about how I didn't belong in Indiana. Would I also find a partner who wanted me *and* understood me? Two big conundrums.

The dreams for a gay man in such a conservative state and environment seemed so limited to me. Besides, Zach and only a few other close friends understood my past.

One of my biggest fears (if not the biggest) is not being understood. This is when you feel hopelessly estranged from the rest of humanity. The isolation of this can break you. Often, there is no blame to slap on someone for a lack of understanding pieces that are exclusively yours—it comes from some shade of trauma that pulled you apart from other human beings. It can literally come from a place or moment in time when you were alone, abused. You were taken from normalcy, and the sooner you get dropped back into normalcy, the better chance you have of reuniting with yourself and others. It's the best way I can explain the "hole." Those who have survived long periods of abuse have this cross to bear. The need to be understood may be greater than other needs because the hole has widened, threatening to swallow other important pieces of ourselves that are met.

With years of therapy, I believe much of my need to be understood stems from the number of times I was denied any ounce of understanding when trying to report the abuse. It corroded my physical health. I went to the cardiologist every six weeks for high blood pressure and an abnormal heartbeat, which I am still treating today, as I mentioned. The abuse had taken its toll on my heart, the one part of my body I so desperately wanted to keep intact for that special someone.

On top of these fears, I also realize that I am extremely dynamic, a passionate person who is always "on," a trait that has opened many doors for me but doesn't always gel with people in certain situations. We all know that too much of a good thing can become a detriment. I'm still navigating how to find the sweet spot between my fiercely passionate nature and coming across as too intense and overzealous. This combination didn't make it easy to find someone to enjoy my life with. At least I had become more self-sufficient, was in school, and my life was on the right path with my chosen family.

Then THE ONE entered my life. In the most sublime way. Electronic music, sunshine, cool breeze.

When I was twenty-four, I met Matt at a music festival in Miami that raised hundreds of thousands of dollars for LGBTQ rights. Thousands of people attended each year. Never in my wildest dreams did I imagine looking at someone across the beach and in an instant, magnetically connect.

Not only was he drop-dead gorgeous with spiked blond hair, ocean blue eyes, and a warm, broad smile—Matt was one of the most brilliant people I had ever met; he was finishing his doctorate degree while concurrently serving as an associate dean of students at a university. One of the first pieces of information that my brain latched onto was that he is classically trained in piano. As much as he and I both loved music, was I dreaming? He also lived in Atlanta, which I was happy to relocate to if/when things progressed up for us. I think my willingness to move also helped us give this relationship a possible go, even long distance.

Amazingly, I would have my answer on where we were on the thermometer within a few weeks. Matt attended a conference that happened to be in Indianapolis. We were inseparable. Official notice: He was mine!

The first time he came to my house, we started talking about work. As I opened my computer to play music, Matt saw that I was looking for a job, which I know could have been a big turnoff.

Instead, as he later told me, he couldn't help but notice the tons of tabs open, jobs, resumé, and applications. He was encouraging and engaging. He didn't judge me. I told him about the interview I had the next morning, for a dream position in the energy industry. And just like that, overnight, with Matt as my lucky charm, I got that job working in legal and compliance for an electricity grid operator, starting my foray in the green energy industry.

Matt and I saw each other every weekend for nine months while we were long distance. Every weekend, we would explore a new city together: a weekend in Montreal, the jazz festival in New Orleans, driving up to Chicago to see friends. I finally found someone as passionate about traveling the world as yours truly!

Right before graduation, I applied for a job at a company in DC that maintained a location in Atlanta. I couldn't stand one more day living apart from Matt (and still in Indiana, at that). Like fairy dust sprinkled on us, I received an offer from the Atlanta office before I even graduated with a degree.

Being the Southern gentleman he is, Matt flew to Indianapolis on a one-way ticket to help me pack up my things. In fact, he alone packed up my belongings in the car because I had two final exams that night. When I returned, smiling broadly, he told me we were hitting the road. Think Celine Dion's song, "Drove All Night!" Eight hours. With every show tune you can imagine. Some classical music. Steak and Shake.

I kept looking in his eyes because I couldn't get enough of what I saw. What did I see? That I was WANTED. I told everyone. I couldn't contain myself.

Leaving my chosen family behind, namely Zach, his then boyfriend Jacob, Don, Beth, and a few other close friends, was only hard because I knew I'd miss them. But they also knew I needed to spread my wings a little and fly. Zach adds: "When you met and eventually moved to Atlanta with Matt, I experienced a range of emotions. I was so happy for you because I knew you belonged somewhere outside of Indiana, but I was selfishly devastated in losing the proximity to my best friend. I knew, however, in my heart, that our bond and friendship was so strong, distance would never drive us apart (and it never did)."

My chosen family expanded. And I was on the fluffiest Cloud 9.

CHAPTER 14

Bliss and Bloodlines

"A man in love is incomplete until he
has married. Then he's finished."

—*Zsa Zsa Gábor*

I worked out the elaborate plan of how Matt would propose to me
in Los Angeles on New Year's Eve. All it takes is a little persuasion.
But I knew he was already planning to propose to me, as he had
enough wits about him to let me pick out our wedding bands prior.
Fast forward to a hot, sweaty July day in Atlanta, and just like that,
we tied the knot! Having no family, I was worried about the need
to live up a traditional wedding, given that Matt has two loving
parents, three siblings, nieces and nephews, and dozens of cousins.

Matt planned everything to be so special: a small, intimate wedding with his parents and siblings on his side, and my chosen family
filed in next to me.

For our honeymoon, pure bliss. Barcelona and Seychelles, just
enough big city fun, sightseeing, and then time at a quaint LGBTQ

friendly beach town. It was a honeymoon precisely for us, and we were living and loving every minute of it.

Then as if the sand and stars were watching us, and in that moment, old and new worlds of mine decided to collide and mix things up. My mother—the real one—contacted me on Facebook. *On. My. Honeymoon.* The last time I saw her had been twenty years before, and I still assumed she was dead. Of all times in twenty years. She bombarded me with questions.

"Were you born on November 4, 1989?"

"Were you born in New Castle, Indiana?"

"What was your mother's name?"

I was sitting in paradise in Barcelona, in love, and married. It was my honeymoon! I was thinking, *this woman has audacity.* First, she spelled my name incorrectly. Did she remember giving my name only one "T"? Then she didn't know if it was me or not. She didn't recognize me. I was born on her birthday. And how many Connie's are out there?

She could have found me earlier. I'd lived in the same small town for all the time she was missing. Twenty years of disappointment and estrangement flooded back into my brain in moments. There were a lot of weird coincidences fusing with the night. Two "James Matthews" in Barcelona now married to each other, as family, and so much emphasis on the name, "Connie," since my mother and the legal guardian had the same name. My mother calling on this night.

My active imagination, slight intoxication, and rampant emotions didn't do me any favors. You can be in paradise and your mind can take you to hell. My mind relived my entire childhood, with my sparkling new husband waiting for the air to clear. I had dealt with most of my trauma in years of therapy. Simultaneously, I didn't have to contemplate my painful past in the new life I created. Until the intrusion.

I slid into a deep fog, haze, for what felt like hours, but Matt said was only a few minutes. Coming to my senses, I replied to my mother, with the only response I could muster. "You gave me away to Connie."

She replied, "But I'm your mother. Will you see me now? I was drunk and tried to get you back. She would not let me have you."

This little chit chat may sound forced, but it was just that blunt. No apology or real explanation. Did she remember that I told her about the abuse when she came back all those years ago? That she lost me again by getting a DUI when she was supposed to be supervising me and winning me back from Connie? That I'd been alone for fifteen years?

Shaking and blurry-eyed, I clumsily informed her that I was on my honeymoon. That I had been in New Castle, in the same school system she left me in. Sitting there on the beach, I noticed Matt staring at me wide-eyed, his blue eyes looking like darting lasers in the moonlight. He was as shocked and speechless as me, wanting to help but knowing through his understanding of me that all I needed in the moment was love, support, and time.

Six months later, she wrote me again: "I want you to meet your brother and sister. I've been clean for a long time. I want to get to know the man you turned out to be. I'm a stay-at-home mom and my wife works at Wal-Mart. I hope you don't take what I did to you out on your brother and sister because they're only eight and ten years old."

So, my mom was gay, too…and she had more kids, even after all that hell I went through? It was a bit too much to swallow.

Her random Facebook messages go back to 2016. Then holiday messages. In between well-wishes, other information trickled out like tainted water from a rusty faucet. Three possible fathers. Then five half-brothers and who knows how many stepbrothers.

One morning, from 23 and Me, a cousin contacted me with family questions and pointed out my father, "Charlie," right there in the family tree. Finally, I knew for sure who my biological was— genetically proven. He had died a few years after I moved to Atlanta.

My name was even in his obituary that Beth sent me, which is almost satiric since his name is not on my birth certificate!

As I chewed on this information in the middle of countless nights, always unable to sleep, I was rising in my career and on the self-help train for becoming a strong leader. And I had my chosen family. I didn't need or want my bloodline.

CHAPTER 15

Revelations with Boys of Ipanema

"The real voyage of discovery consists not in seeking new landscapes but in having new eyes."

—*MARCEL PROUST, NOVELIST*

WITH THE DOOR wide open to my childhood and the chapters of this horror novel that simply contact from my mother instigated, Matt was patient with me every step of the way as I dug up and shared all that I had walled off. Packed deep down were scars and wounds that therapy only put a Band-Aid on. Don't get me wrong. These cover-ups help to move on to be productive and even thrive. But they may shoot sharp pains when depression or anxiety flares up for other reasons. The scars from childhood may always be there as reminders of rejection and fears of abandonment and abuse.

I am not alone in this experience. Even with an amazing life, previous times jump into the present, creating kind of a mishmash of life.

In 2016, Matt and I were on a cruise, and we bonded with a wonderful group of friends from Brazil. Their warmth and passion for life was contagious. After watching on TV the opening ceremony at the Summer Olympics taking place in Rio de Janeiro, the sensual, bright culture drew us to visit a few months later. Over a series of trips, we fell in love with this astonishingly open and warm country. We always stay in Ipanema, Rio's crown jewel where you're able to bask in both the gorgeous sunrise and the sunset on the same beach. The beaches are picturesque, and the emotional revelations…wow!

Brazil as a country has its own challenges that we've observed firsthand and experienced through friends. In the last few years, authoritarian-style political leadership and corruption in the country has continued to exacerbate the separation between the uber rich and the poor. It consistently boasts one of the top ten economies in the world, yet dozens of billionaires and celebrities split the lion share layers above a struggling middle class and 20% of the population living below the poverty line, twice that of the US.

From the location we typically stay in, we have a front-row view of each of these populations in the landscape since some of the *favelas*, or communities typically with very high levels of poverty, are located directly along the hillsides surrounding the beaches. In these areas, we could not help but notice everywhere we went, people were singing and laughing while doing work many Americans would balk at. The street sweeper singing at the top of his lungs while working to keep the streets of his beautiful country clean. The grandmother opening her small coffee stand on the street corner, her whole family there to help in every way they could and go out of their way to make anyone off the street feel welcome. The attendants on the beach whom we would talk to, usually through the help of one of our friends who could translate Portuguese to English and tell us stories of their families in the favelas and the joy they find in life. One homeless person we met who weaved palm leaves into these amazing hats sat and talked with us for over an hour and cried when we gave him a sizable tip just to say "thank you and Happy New Year."

Finding happiness in the smallest of things, and internalizing and emitting the joy of what you can see around you, was one of the biggest revelations of my life. It made me ponder a lot about what made me keep going. How in the world could I have persevered like this, through all my own trauma? Something about our travels here always made me question that.

Sounds like another vacation, but I was truly on a mission to organize a trip for New Year's celebrations as 2019 rang into 2020. I wanted to help my chosen family take a break from school and work, expand their horizons culturally, and understand all they could about the country we've learned so much from, both through its beauty and its shortcomings. I also could never have known that the infectious coronavirus, COVID-19, which had already been detected in Wuhan, China, would creep into every country and thwart further travel plans.

Matt and I had been to Brazil many times now, but I felt an urgency that I couldn't pinpoint. I wanted to make the most of our ten days away from everything.

As we prepped for the trip, Matt and I also knew we needed to escape life's hustle and get a lot out of our systems after the stress from the U.S. political environment and social justice issues we'd been fighting for. We knew that 2020 was going to be one of the most consequential years of our lives if we wanted to turn around the direction of mere basic human dignity in how we work with others. We knew we had to come back from this vacation ready to dive deep into political engagement in Georgia and make as much of a difference as we could in the outcome of key races in our home state. Little did I know this was going to be yet another revolutionary trip for me.

I was walking home with Matt from the beach and there it was—a truck, much like the one me and my mom lived out of when

I was six. I had not seen one like it since. As we strolled by, I saw someone asleep on a makeshift mattress in the back and what looked like a mom and kid throwing a ball together outside of it, laughing, living that moment as best they could.

My revelations continued. First, finding happiness in the smallest of things. In the moments we can. This vivid picture and flashbacks to my nights of fear in the back of the truck also made me realize that trauma and depression may always be a part of me, but they do not have to hold me captive. They do not have to be all-consuming.

For people who do not struggle with depression, this probably seems obvious and easy. But for someone who battles it, it is a daily, sometimes minute-by-minute war. Sometimes I lose the battle in the moment. This reality has given me a whole new world, many different perspectives from which to think about and talk about life's struggles and successes with Matt, classmates, chosen family, or my therapist. When the feelings of captivity sink back in, I look around to find the most seemingly insignificant thing I can that gives me an ounce of joy.

But these revelations weren't the only ones. I had no clue that a few days later, as we were nearing the end of our trip, *the* revelation that helped me make sense of much of how I persevered finally clicked in my mind.

CHAPTER 16
Seen, Cherished and Protected

"The quest for Love changes us. There is no seeker
among those who search for Love who has not
matured on the way. The moment you start looking
for Love, you start to change within and without."

—*ELIF SHAFAK, NOVELIST*

THE GREATEST REVELATION from that trip before the pandemic was what ultimately motivated me to write my story.

Driving back to our condo in a taxi, winding through the streets of Copacabana and Ipanema beaches, admiring the sun, I found an ounce of joy to pull me out of the depression I was feeling that evening. Matt looked at me and I teared up. Happy at last. A lot of work still to do.

He asked, "Baby, through all your past and the worst you experienced and felt, what kept you going? How on earth did you keep fighting?"

I had never thought about it like that. Still, it took me only a few seconds to conjure up the reason.

"Somehow, deep in my soul, I knew that one day, *someone, somewhere*, would truly love me. Would want me," I replied, tears racing down my face. I hadn't cried like this in years. I recanted my thirty years on Earth with this epiphany: the theme of my life was to exude the brightest light to as many people as possible so that I would be the recipient of that same cosmic love. They say purpose is the breath of life. At six years old, you may not understand the intricacies of having a "purpose" to build your life around, but I felt a knowing, something to keep going toward as everything else stagnated in suffering, even terror at times. I didn't know where the next can lid of food would come from, but I knew someone would want me.

Having his own good cry, Matt encouraged me to share my story with the world. My survival story. Our love story. I vowed to share. The beauty in the notion. Many of us are not born with parents amply equipped to love and care for us. It's kind of ludicrous when you think about it since we, as children, don't simply show up in our own bassinette and demand to be cared for.

When I disclosed everything about my childhood, allowing the details to spill forth and then overflow, I realized that person—the one who would, in every sense, love me for who I was, trauma and depression and all, was Matt. It took love from people like Mrs. Hubbard, Beth, Marissa and Marisa, Don, Zach, and myself to prepare me to truly accept his love. Mind you, these connecting dots came together six years into our relationship.

Matt experienced a series of emotions. There was a long pause between us as the words set in like a permanent encyclopedia entry for our special relationship. I had no idea how much this trip would impact my friends, too.

By this time, Zach and his boyfriend, Jacob, had both graduated from college, moved out of Indianapolis and into our spare bedroom in Atlanta. They were settled into new careers and a fabulous life. We couldn't stand going on anymore huge trips without our best friends, so we were insistent they join us that year to make friends from all over the world, air-tour Rio de Janeiro, attend a festival on top of Sugar Loaf Mountain, and wake every day to magnificent views.

My chosen family. Without them and their love (though I may not have seen it as "love" earlier in my life), I question if I'd have survived. Matt's immediate family had fully embraced me, his mother even referring to me as "son" at every turn. His brother, sisters and father are keenly interested in who I am and what I do.

Love takes all forms. In fact, English is one of the few languages in the world that has only one word to describe the concept of love. Other languages have ten, some more than 100, ways to talk about the love in the world and connection and joy that it brings.

I saw happy tears in Zach's eyes often on that trip. We shared the same kind of hell as children, but in the end, we didn't allow it to be all-consuming. We were here, thousands of miles away from rural Indiana.

Zach explains, "The overwhelming theme of these experiences that I shared with my best friend was a powerful factor that helped to fight the one enemy that had plagued me through my entire life: my own anxiety and self-doubt. Not just having these experiences, but sharing them with my best friend, who helped me emphasize and truly embrace every moment, and put life in context for me that everything is and always will be 'okay'. I joke, but the truth of the matter is, if it weren't for you and our chosen family, I would likely be working in some low-wage job, fighting my way through different shifts just to get through the workday so I could live a life that I never truly got any joy out of, never wanted, and that never allowed me to contribute anything positive to the world. This may be an exaggeration. But neither of us would be where we are without the other holding each other up."

In turn, during this same emotion-filled all-nighter together where I had really found the secret for what had kept me going for so long, Matt, too, opened up about the quest for love and belonging, emphasizing various difficult relationships in his life that I didn't know much about. Having come from such a great family (seriously, one of the best!) with so many opportunities afforded to him, he still needed to learn how to reframe situations, pick out the best of life's circumstances and think about his inner strength. He talked about feeling bad about being vulnerable about his own life when so many others have it such harder. But none of us fully comprehend another's struggles, and his vulnerability further propelled our relationship and I know our ability to effect positive change going forward.

Like me, though we came from opposite ends of family dynamics, he had to find self-love and be proud of himself. Love and pride his family and friends had always shown him, but he had yet to accept. Pride is an interesting concept for our kind! Here, Matt had helped me make this trip happen for so many of our friends and worked on colossal causes with the Human Rights Campaign and political movements for well over a decade. He had already influenced so much positive change in our communities and national politics, but I realized that he didn't feel pride for his accomplishments. That part of the reason he was exhausted going into this trip was his own lack of appreciation of what *he* has been able to do and use that as energy for what I knew he could continue to do.

A little too sarcastically, I quipped, "Do you know what 'pride' means?"

His blue eyes shined innocently against the night sky. "Of course..." he stumbled. "Okay, maybe not," he continued.

Matt shared, "I've never let myself feel pride. I usually have thought of pride as too self-centered or egotistical. But then I think about how good of a life I've had, how much worse others have it, and I think about my own not-good deeds in my past and I just, I just don't know what feeling proud of myself even looks like."

I was referring to self-affirmation, dignity, equality, not to mention our wide visibility as a population. What an individual feels when they allow themself some depth of pride boosts self-esteem, mental health, sense of purpose and accomplishment. In the LGBTQ community, we even have whole events called pride—time that we take to celebrate who we are, what we've accomplished, increasing support to fight for more equality, and just live and be ourselves at least for a few days. This is everything to be proud of! Celebrations, parades, and the like are simply a display of that collective pride.

Reflecting with Matt, he had a lot of "a-has" around feelings like pride and associated shame or guilt and resolved to see a therapist about it.

No matter who you are, you should work to find pride in yourself. That love you deserve to give yourself, even if others may not show it. Pride can be in the moments, perhaps being proud of yourself for accomplishing one small goal on a day you're consumed with depression. Love in the simplest of things, giving yourself the extra minutes you need in bed or treating yourself to something you enjoy is because you can, and should. You don't have to feel guilty for feeling proud.

Matt finally replied: "For gay and trans people, the most marginalized people, there is a distinct commonality. We all hunger for that love and acceptance that is denied us for an extended period in our lives, some for decades others even their whole life. No matter if your family was protective and loving, you're longing for some level of acceptance for just *who* you are. Just for *being*. It takes longer in life for some of us to figure that out. People want love and belonging. You are a living incarnation of everything Brené Brown talks about— the power of love, belonging, and vulnerability!"

Staring into that sun, I also set out to fight for our planet more vigorously and to give everything I had to the 2020 political races ahead.

CHAPTER 17

Decoding Politics, Depression and Empathy

"Having anxiety and depression is like being scared
and tired at the same time. It's the fear of failure but
no urge to be productive. It's wanting friends but
hating to socialize. It's wanting to be alone but not
wanting to be lonely. It's caring about everything,
then caring about nothing. It's feeling everything
at once, then feeling paralyzingly numb."

—Unknown (but widely shared!)

Through the revelations I described, interestingly, they occurred during a four-year battle with depression. My romantic heart and maturing identity as an activist for the LGBTQ community, for racial justice, and for the environment could not stop the trauma of four years of hatred, bigotry, and supremacy brutally grinding into our lives between 2016 and 2020.

We may disagree politically, but I must share how the "politics" impact all of us. We may not feel a decision personally, but someone in our lives, whether a coworker or loved one, is always affected.

Disorder and depravity were constant themes, where nearly every policy or law was designed to take something away from our most vulnerable, most marginalized, and benefit the wealthiest amongst us.

Michelle Goldberg's opinion piece for *The New York Times*, "The Mental Health Toll of Trump-Era Politics," was published in January 2022, and wow, what a reminder of my own mental hell. She mentions a study from Kevin B. Smith, chair of the political science department at the University of Nebraska, Lincoln.

"Politics is a pervasive and largely unavoidable source of chronic stress that exacted significant health costs for large numbers of American adults between 2017 and 2020," writes Smith in "Politics Is Making Us Sick: The Negative Impact of Political Engagement on Public Health During the Trump Administration."

"The 2020 election did little to alleviate those effects and quite likely exacerbated them."

She goes on to say that around 40 percent of Americans, he found, "consistently identified politics as a significant source of stress in their lives." Shockingly, about 5 percent to the point of considering suicide in response to political developments.

For me, it started on Election Night in 2016. Whether you voted for her or not, it is hard to dispute, truly dispute, the brilliance and the experience of Hillary Clinton. I believe some of the work she did in Arkansas on early childhood education and ushering through sweeping insurance availability for 12 million+ children, the Children's Healthcare Insurance Program (CHIP), were striking accomplishments dulled by a massive smear campaign against one of the most successful women in politics to rise in the last two decades. Again, I believe we need more women in positions of power. I particularly believe we need more women of color in leadership roles. And I, like many, got crushed under the weight of despair that night. That election loss felt personal as an attack by nearly half of all voters on so many things I hold fundamental to society: equity and justice, fairness, lifting the most vulnerable around us, and spreading love, not division.

Little did I know that at age twenty-seven, it would trigger my greatest bout of depression since early adolescence.

I drank more alcohol that night than I can recall, waking up the next morning and flying to Washington D.C. for work where the world felt like walking zombies. I lost all motivation and inspiration as executive orders started taking shape in early in the administration that took a bite out of my soul and from the soul of America. Orders that rolled back transgender children's rights and the rights of transgender people in the military, diminished trans identities as invalid through Title VII rule changes, actively promoted LGBTQ discrimination under the very flawed guise of "religious liberty," and stripped away access to healthcare for millions. Then we saw white supremacists march in Charlottesville under Donald Trump's name and his banner. And no, under no circumstance are there "good people" on both sides of a KKK rally.

Based on her book, *Self-Care Rx*, which includes her personal story of entrapment in a relationship with a narcissist for eight years, Danielle DonDiego, DO, MBA, concurs with this extension—or reawakening—of trauma.

She writes, "With the U.S. political climate and handling of COVID-19 in 2020 and going into 2021, narcissism was at the root of a world leader's pathology. The entire country underwent abuse from a narcissist, and people were in different stages of this relationship: in love, confused, rejected, anxious, threatened. In addition to this, domestic violence and being cooped up with abusers in individual households compounded the issue for those in violent home situations. Racism was also rooted in this narcissism, with the entire Black community gaslighted and minimized systemically and overtly by some. This was also the case with how immigration was treated, enforcing supremacy and punishment of those that don't fit without giving any solid solution.

"I'm sorry to say, but I feel strongly that we were all in a collective abusive relationship. And this is because a white man of power (like my ex) was able to play his cards to get ahead and blame others for his shortcomings, at all costs. I felt retraumatized hearing the rhetoric, gaslighting and blame shifting occurring on the news daily. I found it's painful to discuss this with anyone who isn't aware what a narcissist is or looks like, because they are very charming and convincing humans. I isolated myself as much as I could, but my physical reaction and nausea to even hearing his voice was evident. Let me just state for the record, even if I had agreed with all views and policies, being retraumatized came from a visceral place, psychological maturity based on previous experience—not politics. Though the political position that holds such massive power over others opens the door to endless 'supply' for the narcissist."

Well, that perfectly sums it up!

I don't know about you, but I feel more validated and constructive in my thinking when a doctor (and one courageously sharing her own experience, at that) speaks the same sentiments.

I both thank and blame the news and social media. I personally believe the world is becoming a better place, every day, especially now because so many wrongs that could not be seen or understood before are getting national attention. Black Lives Matter, finally giving Black and Brown people the opportunity to show the unmistakable police brutality to the world through firsthand video. Images of children in cages at the border reminded me of being tied up, depraved of any standard of decent living conditions. Utterly homeless.

Punished for attempting a shot at a better life.

For several years, this cycle repeated itself every day. Obsessed with news, tearing up or getting visibly angry at every other story, every attack, the next few years were a blur. A lot of therapy. A lot of mornings with such deep depression I didn't want to get out of the bed.

Something awoke in me in the middle of 2018. I was still struggling, but I knew that I had to make a difference through political action. My husband, Matt, serves on several governing boards and is on the National Board of Directors for one of the nation's largest LGBTQ nonprofits, Human Rights Campaign (HRC). His passionate engrossment has opened my eyes to the full breadth of what equality and justice represent currently—where we started, how far we've come, and where we still need to go to make the world a better place for the next generation. I was motivated almost every day, with every phone call or postcard or protest or fundraiser I helped Matt and other local leaders with.

When we woke up the morning after midterm elections in 2018, when Democrats took control of the House (with a record number of female reps, I might add), we had a glimmer of hope that the future we longed for might once again be possible.

Little did I also know that the series of trips to Brazil during this deep depression were what it would take to help me close serious emotional scars and deep wounds, understand *why* and *how* I had made it this far, and resolve to work even harder in 2020.…Then a pandemic.

When COVID-19 blasted through the universe, it was overwhelming for everybody. We burned through food deliveries, immediately sanitizing the boxes the food came in, putting the food on the plate, and sanitizing everything again. As the science was evolving, we had no idea how serious this would become. On top of that, we were going through the beginnings of the long U.S. Presidential election stretch. I lost a lot of sleep. Through all this stress, my anxiety and depression got even worse, and my food and wine residuals were there to show for it.

Then I realized I couldn't eat and drink my way to greatness, as had been reinforced in the early days of AA. My job responsibilities

were only increasing. Graduate classes became more and more difficult, requiring me to have a sharp mind. Simultaneously, Joe Biden
and Kamala Harris would not get elected with me and others known
for pulling our weight in this state responding to chaos with another
plate of tacos and beer instead of *being the change*. I had to start
working toward my goals again: Work out, sleep well, be the change
the world needs from your generation. Treat my mental health and
depression/anxiety by seeking help, unafraid and unashamed as best
I could.

Matt was learning how to help me, how to be an even better
partner trying hard to understand me and my experiences, my anxiety, and my depression. My husband grew up with a very loving
mother, father, siblings, cousins, aunts, and uncles. He had a tre-
mendous support network as far as family goes. He never expressed
sorrow for me not having the same, as he instinctively knew that I
abhorred that response because it's the very response from people
that I always fought to avert. Sympathy tends to seep in as pity.
Pity comes from a narrative of personifying weakness and a lack of
trying; from a position of "less than." That couldn't be my story. I
will take your empathy and compassion, resonance, and solidarity.
Not sympathy. This is one of the many ways I knew he was "the one"
on day one and that only grew stronger with time.

Matt explains, "Once I reframed your experience in my own
head, I could appreciate everything, all the joy and value you
bring to my life and to the world around me every day. I believe in
karma—the idea that we receive back the good we put out in the
world and even if we don't, it's better to put out as much good as you
can rather than the opposite. You, through it all, are a walking, positive karma-producer with the amount of love and positive energy
you put out in the world. Even after all you have been through,
you are constantly doing little things for people to make their day
brighter, easier, happier. To everyone, from a cashier in at the gro-
cery store to a taxi driver to a congressperson. Doesn't matter who

or what they do, you want to show your love. As good of a life as I've had, all the privilege I've been afforded, it is so easy, even still, to get wrapped up in the negative around me. To be weighed down by life. You make people laugh and smile everywhere.

"The pursuit of happiness requires us to find glimmers of hope and happiness in every moment that we can, even when it feels like life is far from it. You have taught me this the most. It doesn't mean we can't be incredibly critical of systems and the status quo, but we need some nugget of happiness. Of pride. Of love. Of joy. We need that to help drive our very own being."

It took Matt a lot of therapy on his own to reconcile all this and learn to be okay with (even if his life was mostly good) being proud of his accomplishments. To struggle. To suffer with some depression himself. And that seeking mental help is so important for all of us. After all, I couldn't be prouder of Matt if I tried.

On the last day of the previous administration's reign, seeing them leave the White House, something flipped in me. A deep desire to do more, learn more, fight more. It's as if the depression flipped. My alcohol consumption was easier to reduce. My eating habits were easier to gain some control over, and I lost thirty pounds within a few months. I know this will not be my last battle with depression. I also know no matter how deep any future pain feels, I can and will persevere.

CHAPTER 18
Fiery, Audacious Mission

"Sooner or later, we will have to recognize that the earth has rights, too, to live without pollution. What mankind must know is that human beings cannot live without Mother Earth, but the planet can live without humans."

—*Evo Morales*, former *President of Bolivia*

In truth, I believe that once I felt wanted and that I belonged somewhere, I could allow myself to care about a larger purpose on this earth and apply my life toward making a difference. For more than half my life, every waking moment had to be focused on myself, my survival, my mental health, my happiness.

At last, I was in a place in my life where I could dream in vivid colors how I might make the world a better place. How I might leverage my past to find and pursue a dream career. Spanning from the racism I witnessed firsthand to the oppression of LGBTQ people, childhood poverty and homelessness, abuse and neglect, and impacts of climate change, I gradually became more and more aware, passionate of these issues and eager to find a way to have a lasting impact on the world.

This fiery, audacious mission has given back to me in the way of more deeply connected relationships. Sometimes fighting for a larger cause seems difficult at first, given that it takes patience and persistence to see the results or rewards matriculate.

Finding your way at work is also easier with a mentor, someone who takes you under their wing and teaches you everything you need to know, especially for children without a parent, guardian, or sibling to trust and lean on. Everyone needs a support system. For millions of children, orphaned and often alone or perhaps just ostracized from their family for being different, a support system is lifesaving.

Serendipitously, I had always been interested in public policy and law since I went through the process of my own battle fighting the court to escape foster care and finished my undergraduate degree. Oh, the long nights working full-time and trying to finish school! Around the time I met Matt, I applied for a position at a company in Atlanta charged with regulating the energy grid and advocating for more efficient regulations, as well as addressing the advance uptake of green energy solutions like wind and solar with new international policy.

Almost nine months later, the call came. I was elated. The interviews felt like a breeze—easier when you're passionate about the subject matter. From then on, I committed myself to the energy sector and clean energy.

I always had a passion for the law, a passion for working with people, and a yearning for finding common ground for the common good. This job melded all three of these passions into one incredible experience, launching me onto an exciting career path.

My best work friend, Jackie, is one reason why I always kept going. She is a brilliant electrical engineer and a UNC Law School alumna. She's mostly responsible for helping me believe in myself in terms of never wasting away to complacency: she had a faith in me, believed in me, that I could develop a stronger sense of self professionally, realize my worth, that I was good enough and could perform at high levels. The imposter syndrome I felt all my life, never sure if I could do it or if anyone would believe in me, was slowly disappearing at work now, thanks to her mentorship. That type of mentorship is something that's hard for spouses or friends to provide; they don't see you in action every day, and unless you work in the same industry or company, can't truly understand the nuances and technicalities of what's going on in your world.

When we first met, we were in a departmental meeting, at opposite corners of a long, narrow conference table. First impressions are important when you are trying to amass a support system to help you further yourself and a cause larger than you.

Jackie offers, "I observed your vitality, and the effect it had on that typically somber group. Rather than becoming further subdued, the other meeting participants responded to the positive force of your *joie de vivre* by becoming engaged in the discussion with you, as well as each other. The mood of the meeting shifted, from a place of silent tolerance, to one of open collaboration. It was a motivating display of the positive impact one can have on others."

To add context, I was simply pointing out good things about people in the company that weren't very popular and observing and *celebrating* that everyone has a different learning style. I believe that this stemmed from lessons learned along the way to find the very best I could in each situation, no matter how tough the going would get.

We became inseparable friends and colleagues, with long hours of her coaching me on the politics of tough work environments, us trading off the roles of good cop and bad cop to lead and influence policy writing teams to churn through extremely technical and legal electrical and energy policy regulations. Boy, did we laugh a lot along the way!

Jackie adds, "We had a lot of weird things happen to us. I think it is our energy together. A happy circumstance, but not entirely unexpected—such good fortune and positive opportunities had become the norm—somehow, even without speaking, your positive influence on others was evident."

I have learned that you can be true to yourself and professional at the same Time. Also, humor and irony are healthy replacements for frustration and anger. This is how I live my life. I always try to find the funny, or at least a glimmer of hope, in even the most ridiculous and hard situations: anyone who has met me will tell you that. One person can positively impact others and change the course of a collaborative effort, while being their true self. Although Jackie is more than fifteen years my senior, we always shared the spotlight. In fact, if someone said, "Good job, Jackie," she would share the credit with me. I did the same. Stronger together!

As I climbed further in a high-stakes industry regulated by an arm of the US Department of Energy, I learned the influence of mentorship and diplomacy daily. One person who represented this package was Stan, a vice president at my company who always pushed for me to know my value within the company and fight for my worth. When I caught the eye of the HR department as an up-and-comer with high potential, Stan started mentoring me. Having Stan as a mentor was a gift, so I wanted to be sure he saw my extraordinarily strong work ethic. It was a regulatory organization representing over 200 full-time employees from Atlanta and Washington, but Stan faithfully advocated for more diversity and inclusion from his position in the tech-business function.

Stan paints the picture of the kind of interaction we had: "You were very comfortable in your own skin. Being a gay man in a very conservative industry and company. For other people it would have been easier to keep a low profile. And others embraced you. I'm a white male, been married almost forty years. From a traditional Southern family, but that you and I could have a productive mentoring relationship says a lot about you. You didn't expect special treatment. You wanted to choose your own path, and you worked hard for what you wanted to achieve. I don't know all the details about your upbringing, but those bad experiences helped to create you and what you could overcome. That is inspirational to me. You are willing to learn from other people. You and your husband have traveled the world. You are open to letting others be a part of your life. You have given me more mentorship than I could have ever given you over the years."

After hearing Stan's words, I kind of lost my breath. I definitely lost my coolness in the moment. I had no idea that our relationship was so reciprocal. I mentored him? While I always aspire to bring my worth to every relationship, it was such a compliment from one of the people to whom I looked up to most, and I relish in the fact that I could have made an impact on his life. This type of affirma-.tion is higher than any prize I could win in life.

I cannot stress enough what a great mentorship can do in your life. People who believe in you when you can't detect a drop of belief in yourself at times.

Jackie is ultimately, with the support of Matt and friends, the reason I am currently finishing up grad school at a top globally ranked Master of Public Administration program at University of North Carolina at Chapel Hill. Jackie consistently reinforced that I had what it takes to always go further. She is the woman who has been arguably the most influential when it comes to furthering my career and higher education. We worked together for about four years as we wrote electric policy for the U.S., Canada, and Mexico.

People call me a rule-follower for working in "compliance." Proud rule follower here—I work for one of the world's largest renewable energy producers, which requires complex rules and reg-ulations, and it's my job to make sure the company is following the rules and regulations across North America.

Green power is the future; we are setting the global standard for it. We produced 34% more clean energy in North America than what was projected for 2020, and my company is based in over thirty countries. While the pandemic raged, I contributed to initiatives that led to several accolades you would never hear about. My company was featured in the 2020 SEAL Organizational Impact Award category, representing the fifty most sustainable companies globally. Our Spanish subsidiary was also among the winners in the same category. The Group ranked first out of 150 Italian companies in the Reputation Science's ESG Perception Index, which evaluates companies' sustainability perception on the web based on their brand's proximity to ESG topics.

When working to ensure all parts of a company understand, value, and apply policy and regulation with the goal of increasing the reliability of our entire electric grid, I have learned that messaging is key, and we must make a lot of points without blame or shame. Growing up a fighter but through all my experiences, somehow navigating these types of politics became easier. It makes me think back around the persuasion I learned at an early age.

My current fierce, fabulous boss is a multi-racial woman, and let me tell you this: we need more people of color in positions of power, especially women of color. She is an amazing mentor. She is a natural-born leader, so being under her wing has opened doors I'd never known existed. But this relationship has really shown me the value of upward mentorship as well. I do everything I can to encourage my team and advocate for others to speak up or speak out in a variety of tough settings. But we love what we do, and we know that climate challenges are social justice challenges.

Why is this important?

The issues that squelch our potential as a society are intertwined, as I mentioned before. Not every company is solely driven by profit. Sure, many are but there are a lot that do really good work in the world now. The dramatic effects of climate change have much wider, far-rippling effects, especially on less fortunate people around the globe. The exacerbation of entire forests and wetlands, forcing some of the poorest in the world to die or find a way to move thousands of miles. We see the increasing severity of hurricanes and tornados, year after year, destroying the poorest areas of coastlines and islands around the world and often poorer stretches of the Midwest US. Climate change *is* a racial justice issue of our time with these disasters disproportionally hurting Black, LatinX, and indigenous communities in the U.S. and around the globe.

I'm not suggesting all white people are less impacted or that there isn't rampant poverty there, too. The effects overall transcend race but still have a disproportionate affect.

With this experience, I aspire to work in positions in international policy to advocate the values of equality abroad, perhaps working for an ambassador in the State Department. I am an ambassador for whatever I do: model the behavior you want to see in other people. There is a responsibility. We can't commit compliance violations and ensure the company is in a positive light. We still have a lot of work to do to attract and retain more women in energy, and my company is working on diversity, equity, and inclusion initiatives I participate in.

An impactful, eye-opening activity for me in graduate school was a leadership class I took. Honestly, when was the last time you thought about your vision for your life, your stance as a leader or contributor, and were forced to take the time to reflect on that? Sure, the homework may have been a challenge with working full-time, but the exercise helped shed so much light for me as a leader. The act of writing out my own personalized vision for leadership gave me motivation.

As my teacher reflected and taught us, writing it down helps you gain clarity (and writing it down makes the picture more easily seen by others). In a lot of leadership theories, empathy is not always inherent or a central tenant but for me, it is. Empathy can be magnetic, however, if you are vulnerable enough to share your truth, and vulnerability is a hallmark of great leaders. If you possess clarity, the picture is easily seen by others. The following is the vision/mission statement I wrote for my graduate Public Service Leadership course taken in 2021. I share it as an example of the clarity that I gained through the process. After all I had been through, I was proud of my work.

My vision for leadership circles on energy and the inspiration we can give each other as leaders. I hope to be a spark of lightning to others in all aspects of life. I lead by ensuring that my proverbial circuit breaker is strong and resolute with protecting my electrical circuit (friends, family, colleagues, etc.) while allowing as much current to flow as possible, preserving the balance. I am rejuvenated by others' energies, and I strive to be a positive energy to anyone when I walk into the room: both by supporting others' passions and energy in the room, as well as ensuring that my positive energy serves to energize those whose energy needs a productive boost.

The future I have envisioned is to continue shining my light to others as well as showing others the transformative leader I strive to be, given that I have overcome so many obstacles. The quality that makes my envisioned future distinctive is just that— that energy is in 100 percent of my life both figuratively and literally. My job is to instill others to be passionate about sustainable energy while adhering to strict federal regulations regarding power markets.

My title contains the word, 'reliability', and I strive to show others that I am both reliable and consistent, much like the continental electrical grid. This is what my image of leadership is like: a tall, sturdy, enormous wind turbine generator, just one part of large windfarm. That turbine generates electricity all on its own, but it takes a field—often dozens or hundreds—of other turbines to come together at a common point where it aggregates before being put transmitted the electric grid. This is because some turbines on the same farm may get wind from various angles and speeds, some turbines may have a better day than others, but collectively they have to ensure a steady output onto the grid. Individual leadership.

Collective impact.

This vision reinforces the fact that I love to (and think it is best to) lead by the 'power of our example' and not the 'example of our power' as our forty-sixth President has noted throughout his life. While I may be just one turbine amongst hundreds in the wind farm, I am still needed with the teamwork of the others. I think back to the worst blackout in North America (2003) where the cascading blackouts were caused by companies' negligence when working together for the reliability of the grid. My light in the future is much like the spark to prevent such blackouts from occurring as we all work together.

Long-term trends and potential future developments relating to my vision are to continue to learn more and more about the electric utility industry, how to continue generating more green power, and combine this with my passion for public service and global sustainability. I also am very passionate about politics and understand that my constituents will not only be those with whom I work but the community as a whole.

At an early age, I realized that I was a natural leader, but I never felt proud of myself. Ironic, right, after helping Matt dig deep into his own issues of pride and self-esteem? Receiving a title next to my name never mattered. The traits that make an empathetic leader did though. I struggled with imposter syndrome, never living up to the expectations I set for myself. I was busy climbing out of the abyss. But others saw and see it in me. It is empowering when you feel alignment in how you are perceived (positively!) and how you feel.

CHAPTER 19

Owning My Story and the Difference I Will Make

"Don't ask yourself what the world needs. Ask yourself what makes you come alive—and go and do that. Because what the world needs is people who have come alive."

—*Howard Thurman*

WHY DID I want to tell my story now? I'm not famous. I have much work to do on myself and on finding ways to keep making a difference in the world. Honestly, it has taken me these thirty-two years to reconcile what happened to me, live out parts of my life to explore who I am and what I want, and find security. I'm one of the lucky ones. But if I waited until I was seventy to write a motivational memoir, there may have been thirty-five years missed of inspiring some kid to make it through their own situation, or to inspire another generation of leaders to fight for positive change for foster and abused children, and repair of the foster care system.

For a large part of my life, I could not even say the phrase, "foster kid," or orphan. One of the hardest journeys for me was reconciling all the negative experiences inside my identity as an orphan, as a foster kid. It took me almost twenty-five years. I hated that part of my identity, and the things society prescribes to being a foster child. I was ashamed. When you're ashamed of a core part of who you are, shame is debilitating. For some of my life, I was ashamed of both my status as an orphan and as a gay kid. Luckily, I had the support structures I needed to overcome shame of being gay much earlier in my life. But shame can decimate your life by throwing up so many roadblocks and is only exacerbated by continually closing doors. Rejection, isolation, pain. Those are the clenchers. Then before you know it, you're hiding or withdrawing from reality and from the possibility of a better tomorrow. That's not living.

I was, indeed, a foster kid. It was the hand I was dealt by a single parent who was an addict. Fact. I now can own my story, and owning your full story is empowering. I finally feel pride in my story.

The dream to be *wanted, to be loved unconditionally,* kept me alive, not the care of adults. Throughout my childhood, people failed me along the way. I don't know how but finding a way to reform the system in such a way that seeks to ensure above all else, every child feels loved and wanted, is so critical to me.

What do I want everyone know about foster kids? First, kids are kids. And the developmental advantages of having active parents and guardians is exponential. Children take a great deal into their brains before the age of five, and the more children are exposed to language, are read to, are talked to, the more opportunities they will have throughout their life. Direct statistical relationships exist between simply the number of words children hear early in their life through reading and talking and the long-term likelihood of that child graduating high school or ending up in jail.

There are currently more than 400,000 children in foster care in the United States alone. In 2019, over 672,000 children spent time in U.S. foster care. In 2020, the Children's Bureau of the U.S. Department of Health and Human Services reported that Indiana and Kentucky had child abuse rates more than double the national average. The average age of kids entering the system is actually 8 years old, a lot higher than many would guess. The federal agency's latest "Child Maltreatment" report, which covers incidents reported and investigated in 2017, shows that there were 29,189 victims of child abuse in Indiana alone. That translates to a rate of 18.6 victims per 1,000 children. Nationally, research indicates nearly one in three, or 30 percent, of foster youth experience abuse from guardians/caregivers.

I will always be associated with trying to effect change in the world on this topic. No child should have to deal with what I did. These issues are all intertwined on some level. Poverty and addiction and abuse and racial or sexual orientation injustice drive low self-esteem in too many kids around the country, and these experiences regularly lead to low grades, low opportunities, high suicide rates, human trafficking, and on and on.

An old African proverb reads, "It takes a village to raise a child," and that concept inspired Hillary Clinton to write her award-winning book by a similar name in 1996. She wrote, "We are living in an interdependent world where what our children hear, see, feel, and learn will affect how they grow up and who they turn out to be."

At the time she wrote this book, I was in the throes of physical abuse, daily rejection, and isolation, and had just escaped living in the back of a pickup truck. I am so grateful for the nonprofits that focus on changing policies, bettering organizations, and work hard to oust local and state politicians that created the very systems that failed me, and fail so many others, as homeless, abandoned, and in my case, gay. Yet still too many foster and adoption organizations don't. They put their own religious beliefs and doctrines over the physical, emotional, and psychological wellbeing of children. These types of organizations are often in rural areas or states where being gay or being trans is still not protected by equal protection of the law.

Too often, society places pressures on marginalized people—that they can pull themselves up by their own bootstraps, that their pain and trauma is somehow less "real" and thus, not worthy of investing tax dollars on, that mental health isn't a real thing, that they should just be able to find a job and do better.

That pressure is insurmountable for many people. We must change that together.

I survived. I thrive now through helping others thrive and by advocating for real, systemic change in public policy on these issues.

One thing my friend, Zach, said perfectly speaks to the reason I wrote *Wanted*. "Many of us have 'stories' and come from unique backgrounds that will always shape how we live our lives and impact the world. Some aren't perfect, some are troubled, and some are tragic. But the real story isn't the background of a person, it's how they leverage that background or story to impact the world. We have to conquer the tribulations of the past and use their memory as one of our greatest tools to keep making positive differences in people's lives and in our own."

I have a story of personal mental health, success in my career, and joy in the face of it all. I'm finally proud of that story. My husband and I are on our eighth year together. My career and graduate education are taking off, and I know I will continue to use my persuasion and zest for life to make a difference in the world, especially around foster care reform, LGBTQ equality and adoption challenges, and addressing climate change. I hope each aspect about my life can be used as a sliver of hope and inspiration for someone else to keep going, to keep fighting, to persevere, to seek the help they need. Or for another to take action in their community.

I pray this, in some way, inspires us all to action. To be a part of the village that makes lives better not just for their own families but beyond, as so many are pushed out of, or denied loving childhood learning experiences. I hope I've given you a few nuggets of inspiration to continue your own fight for what you believe in and perhaps another person's experience to tell to cast light on injustice. That my story can make an impact benefitting the plights of children. Gay children. Children of color. Trans children. I pray that my life, that my story, gives us all inspiration. Motivation. Calls us to action. Most importantly, gives you a greater awareness to have true empathy for the challenges we face. Because too many cannot.

At thirty-two years old, with a beard, I see hints of my mother in my face. In January 2020, as explained, my mother started contacting me via text again five years after my honeymoon. I was just re-reading my messages that my mom was the one trying to overdose herself once she found out "they" were going to take me since we were homeless. I thought it was just her being an alcoholic. What that means is that I was coming home from kindergarten and feeding her every day; this was literally saving my mom from suicide. It's my story, and it's the story of thousands of kids, foster and not, in situations of neglect and abuse. The story of millions of kids around the globe.

I held out hope that my mother would give me one hour of reflections and insight for this book and tried to persuade her repeatedly. In this case, I was not persuasive! I hope this doesn't feel like an indictment of her but an indictment of the systems that fail children and a culture that does not elevate mental health.

Alas, she didn't contribute. She simply couldn't. Now, I understand.

Now, I can truly forgive her.

Never-ending Quest for Systemic Reform

I DEBATED LONG and hard about how best to make a case for change while also focusing on my story. So, I decided to add an epilogue that shares further information about three main areas of need for systemic change that were barriers throughout my own life—around being gay, an abused foster kid, and that I know will be a barrier for future generations: climate change.

Owning my story of impact drives me, maybe even requires me, to make commitments. My story is not a story for the faint of heart (the irony is that I personally have heart complications).

Child Abuse, Adoption Law, and Foster Care Reform

One in three. One in three, or 30 percent, of youth in foster care situations will experience abuse and neglect from caregivers. With the number of foster youths rising nationwide, Indiana recently released one of the most detailed reports on how well these students do in school. That makes the state a leader as federal law more recently requires all states to report academic data for these students, and many have yet to comply.

Indiana's report, which includes more than is federally required, confirms just how challenging it is for students in foster care to receive a good education. This first-of-its-kind data set for Indiana finds that graduation rates for these students are more than twenty points lower than the state average and they are falling far behind in reading and math. These students also face high rates of discipline and are more likely to attend failing schools.

But even these dire data points might miss the mark for the true educational outcomes of students in foster care. Advocates say that the state could be undercounting the number of students in foster care by half. Students in foster care who are in special education, or a racial minority perform even worse than their peers. Among the report's findings:

- 64 percent of students in foster care graduate from high school, compared with 88 percent of all students.

- 1 in 5 foster youth don't have to meet all the requirements for graduation to receive a diploma, and fewer than 1 in 10 graduate with academic honors.

- Only 9 percent passed their 10th-grade state math test, while 28 percent passed in reading.

- 3 percent of black students in foster care passed the 10th-grade math exam, and 15 percent passed reading.

- Students who are in both foster care and special education have the lowest pass rate on the state test, at 1 percent and 6 percent in math and reading, respectively.

How many of these children were not believed or were wronged by the justice system favoring bloodlines? If one in three are abused, how much more detrimental is our current system than people realize?

In April 2021, Healthychildren.org, whose content is rigorously vetted by pediatricians, reported that approximately four million cases of child abuse and neglect involving almost seven million children are reported each year. The highest rate of child abuse is in babies less than one year of age, and 25 percent of victims are younger than age three. This information is just jaw-dropping and stomach-sinking to me. Most cases reported to Child Protective Services involve neglect, followed by physical and sexual abuse. There is considerable overlap among children who are abused, with many suffering a combination of physical abuse, sexual abuse, and/or neglect. Not to mention the emotional toll this has on a young person.

The following changes are seen in many children because of many different stressful situations and are not specific to child abuse and neglect, but the reason for the appearance of these behaviors should always be investigated.

- Fearful behavior (nightmares, depression, unusual fears)
- Unexplained abdominal pain, sudden onset of bed-wetting, or regression in toileting (especially if the child has already been toilet trained)
- Attempts to run away
- Extreme sexual behavior that seems developmentally inappropriate for the child's age
- Sudden change in self-confidence
- Headaches or stomach aches with no medical cause
- School failure
- Extremely passive or aggressive behavior
- Desperately affectionate behavior or social withdrawal
- Big appetite and stealing food

I know I displayed multiple signs of abuse besides the actual words that came out of my mouth when crying "abuse," yet adults in positions of authority did nothing…for years. It stabs me inside even today. Not because of what I personally endured, but for the millions of kids that may be suffering needlessly, right at this moment, with their lives and lifelong potential on the line. There seems to be a default tendency in this country to "believe parents." I hope through movements toward believing survivors, which are gaining momentum today, that survivors of childhood abuse are also considered part of the sea change.

LGBTQ Rights and the Fight for Equality

One in three. One in three kids in foster care or up for adoption identify as LGBTQ. The only way forward to a better future is to treat all with respect and equity. As you get to know someone who is gay, you understand sexual orientation more. You can be a better parent to that kid that says they're gay or trans at an early age. The Human Rights Campaign Foundation's All Children All Families program is a great place to start if becoming more educated and engaged is a goal. They report that LGBTQ youth are "over-represented," meaning the percentage of youth in care who identify as LGBTQ is *higher*, significantly, than in the general child population. It's also more disproportionate for transgender children.

HRC reported, "A survey of LGBTQ youth in New York City found:

- 78 percent of LGBTQ youth were removed or ran away from their foster placements as a result of hostility toward their sexual orientation or gender identity.

- 100% of LGBTQ youth in group homes reported verbal harassment.

- 70% of LGBTQ youth reported physical violence in group homes.

This is in *New York City*. Imagine what LGBTQ folks around the country are experiencing. Moreover, some youth enter the foster care system for the same reasons as other children, and many have added layers of psychological impact from experiencing abandonment, rejection, abuse directly related to who they are and who they love.

What drove much of my depression over the four-year span I discussed in Chapter 17? As Human Rights Campaign (HRC) astutely stated, "The Trump-Pence Administration unleashed a torrent of attacks on the LGBTQ community and undermined the rights of millions of Americans. Through rollbacks, rescissions, and re-interpretations, Donald Trump and Mike Pence systematically and meticulously eroded years of progress and protections. What's more, Trump and Pence appointed and nominated scores of extreme and unqualified anti-LGBTQ officials to crucial agencies and court benches—some of whom will serve lifetime appointments. Beyond these extensive, explicit attacks on LGBTQ equality, the Trump-Pence Administration targeted many of the most marginalized within our community—from banning Muslim refugees, to undermining voting rights, to putting the lives and livelihoods of 75,000 LGBTQ 'Dreamers' at risk."

Therefore, I want to capture a snapshot of the discriminatory conduct of the Trump-Pence Administration here. I understand why journalists and documentary filmmakers must show the real images of atrocities like war. Pretty summaries keep others emotionally removed. And emotion incites change. Besides, so much is missed by mainstream media that politicians go unchecked for their deeds. See for yourself.

I shamelessly cite these stats from HRC's website that one U.S. Presidential administration was responsible for. These discriminatory policies have wrecked people's lives:

- Trump and Pence weaponized HHS [US Department of Health and Human Services] to deny life-saving health care to LGBTQ people: The White House announced the creation of a so-called "Conscience Division" at the Department of Health and Human Services to enable medical providers to deny even life-saving health care to LGBTQ people if their personal beliefs conflicted with a patient's sexual orientation and/or gender identity. This could enable hospitals to turn away LGBTQ patients, regardless of the severity of their health care needs.

- Trump moved to reinstate a ban on qualified transgender people serving in the military, which could have resulted in the discharge of more than 15,000 transgender Americans serving our country.

- Trump instructed the DOJ to give federal agencies direction on "interpreting religious liberty protections in Federal law." The Attorney General's directive put millions of LGBTQ Americans at risk of discrimination and to reconsider current and future regulations.

- The DOJ asserted that Title VII doesn't apply to LGBTQ people: The Department of Justice (DOJ) filed an amicus brief arguing that Title VII of the Civil Rights Act of 1964, which prohibits discrimination on the basis of sex, does not protect lesbian, gay, or bisexual people from discrimination. The DOJ rescinded a memo issued by the Obama Administration and replaced it with a discriminatory memo, arguing that Title VII also does not apply to transgender people. DOJ instructed all U.S. attorneys to adopt this dangerous position in all pending and future matters.

- The DOJ and ED put transgender students at risk by rescinding protective Title IX guidance: Under the direction of Attorney General Jeff Sessions and Education Secretary Betsy DeVos, the U.S. Departments of Justice and Education revoked the Obama Administration's guidance detailing schools' obligations to transgender students under Title IX of the Education Amendments.

We must demand of our Republican and Democratic leaders to pass the Equality Act. Core and basic freedoms are missing in over half, twenty-nine, states across the country. These freedoms mean that LGBTQ Americans can be refused service, be denied housing, and experience discrimination in healthcare. Now, think about the even more adverse impacts of these types of freedoms on the plights of LGBTQ youth in foster programs.

Climate Change

A litany of facts on the science of global warming and climate change is overwhelming. But I want to start with the human impact. The United Nations details many alarming impacts:

- An increase in the severity of storms and disasters like hurricanes, droughts, and extreme temperatures over the last three decades is alarming. According to the UN, "There were more than 11,000 reported disasters attributed to these hazards globally, with just over two million deaths and $3.64 trillion in losses. More than 91 percent of the deaths occurred in developing countries." This means the poorest among us in the world are gravely impacted by climate change.

- *National Geographic* reports, "Rising seas is one of those climate change effects. Average sea levels have swelled over 8 inches (about 23 cm) since 1880, with about three of those inches gained in the last 25 years. Every year, the sea rises another .13 inches (3.2 mm). New research published on

February 15, 2022, shows that sea level rise is accelerating and projected to rise by a foot by 2050." So what? "Already, flooding in low-lying coastal areas is forcing people to migrate to higher ground, and millions more are vulnerable from flood risk and other climate change effects. The prospect of higher coastal water levels threatens basic services such as Internet access, since much of the underlying communications infrastructure lies in the path of rising seas."

- Climate change is also a racial Justice issue. Global Citizen details the disproportionate effect of climate change and sea-level rising, flooding, and more on communities of color around the world and right here in the U.S. With Hurricane Katrina, 80 percent of the people who lost their homes were Black. Because racism intertwines socio-economic status, it means that communities of color will be much less likely to be able to move, relocate, etc. as things get worse.

- Weather extremes are decimating crops across the globe. With the world's population expected to exceed 9.5 billion people by 2050, food production both contributes to climate change and will be a real challenge where millions, even billions, in poor countries and poor areas of the US will have less access, if any at all, to basic foods.

Following a calling almost as loud as love and belonging, I landed a position writing electricity policy. Energy and energy production is one of the leading negative impacts on our globe. When you say you "advocate for environmental change," some people still interpret this as sending money to an organization for saving an endangered species up in the trees 5,000 miles away, or recycling some of our garbage in a blue receptacle—no matter if it's plastic or paper—so we know we're "doing our part." But in just the short time since I started writing this book (and enduring a pandemic like the rest of the world), a variety of extreme weather events further demonstrate the impacts, and progression, of climate change. These events, from forest fires to hurricanes with much greater intensity to melting of ice caps, all present the real case for reversing some of the damage that humans have done to the planet—or we simply will not have a livable planet any longer.

According to NASA, the year of 2020 was the warmest year on record. Massive wildfires scorched Australia, Siberia, and the United States' West Coast, making it the most active fire season on record, and many of the fires were still burning during the busiest Atlantic hurricane season on record. In addition, 23.1 million square kilometers of Greenland's ice sheet (about 70 percent of the ice sheet's surface) reached the melting point. Glaciers and mountain ice caps in places like Alaska, South America, and High Mountain Asia are continuing to melt, contributing more than either Greenland or Antarctica to sea level rise, which affects coastal communities around the world. These events are likely the consequence of decades of greenhouse gas emissions.

In sum, the current warming trend is of particular significance because it is unequivocally the result of human activity since the mid-20th century and proceeding at a rate that is unprecedented over millennia, asserts the Intergovernmental Panel on Climate Change (IPCC), which includes thousands of scientists with the greatest experience in climate change research and which publishes the authoritative scientific assessments of climate change. Prior to these more recent apocalyptic scenarios (the photos say it all), I was swayed to get involved by massive blackouts, leaving people stranded in elevators and subways or without air conditioner to the point of dying from heat stroke because of an outdated power infrastructure. Not to mention all the people who have perished in hospitals and assisted living facilities.

Wanting a Better Future, Demanding a Better Future

There is so much that can be done. **"Never doubt that a small group of thoughtful committed individuals can change the world. In fact, it's the only thing that ever has,"** is one of my favorite quotes by Margarete Mead.

One day, Matt and I will investigate fostering or adopting, though I'm not fully sure I can be a parent yet, if ever. That may be one way to make change. There are so many others. Consider participating in a local Big Brother- or Big Sister-style mentoring program for at-risk youth. Deeply search your own personally held convictions and how those, even of the best intentions, may have unintended impacts or consequences that hurt so many others. Reflect on how that translates into your votes. Find a local non-profit to volunteer at. Give of your treasure to organizations like the HRC Foundation, NAACP, Planned Parenthood, or myriad local organizations in your backyard.

After all, real change requires national, system-level transformation *and* local, individualized work. Matt and I have attended so many LGBTQ advocacy events. We've given financial support and raised millions in funds with other supporters. We've lobbied at the U.S. Capitol for racial and LGBTQ equality, and healthcare legislation. We bring our own professional knowledge to every table for change. We organize get-out-the-vote campaigns and knock-on countless doors promoting pro-equality political candidates in coalition with local organizations. It's wonderful to be married to a fellow change-maker. To finally embrace my own story and to use it for change.

I learned from watching Matt that fighting for social justice goes beyond posting opinions on social media. Democracy demands on-the-ground advocacy, not passively posting for Instagram likes. Our conversations are spritely! But what matters most is our unwavering goal of making a difference. If we pave a different way, expose the wrongs, and set an example for what's right, we can wake up each day to a brighter sunrise. No matter where we are in the world.

References

Interviews

Matt Garrett. In-person interview. January 26, 2020.

Stan Hoptroff. Zoom interview. July 1, 2020.

"Jackie." Written interview. May 29, 2020.

Zach Johnson. Written interview. June 24, 2020.

"Joseph and Sheila." Written interview. August 10, 2020.

Beth McKechnie. Written interview. May 29, 2020.

Don Young. Phone interview. June 23, 2020.

Publications

American Academy of Pediatrics. "Caring for Your Baby and Young Child: Birth to Age 5." Healthychildren.org. Updated April 8, 2021.

https://www.healthychildren.org/English/safety-prevention/at-home/Pages/What-to-Know-about-Child-Abuse.aspx

Chatterjee, Rhitu. "How Trauma Affects Memory: Scientists Weigh in on the Kavanaugh Hearing." *NPR.org.* September 28, 2018.

https://www.npr.org/sections/health-shots/2018/09/28/652524372/how-trauma-affects-memory-scientists-weigh-in-on-the-kavanaugh-hearing

DonDiego, Danielle. *Self-Care Rx.* Atlanta, Georgia: Self-Care Rx, LLC. July 13, 2021.

The Editors of Encyclopedia. Britannica. "Lantern Festival." *Britannica.* December 15, 2021.

https://www.britannica.com/topic/Lantern-Festival

Goldberg, Michelle. "The Mental Health Toll of Trump-Era Politics." The New York Times. January 21, 2022.

https://www.nytimes.com/2022/01/21/opinion/trump-politics-mental-health.html

History.com Editors. "Patrick Henry." History.com. Updated March 18, 2021.

https://www.history.com/topics/american-revolution/patrick-henry

Human Rights Campaign. "The Trump-Pence Administration's Crusade Against LGBTQ Americans."

https://assets2.hrc.org/files/assets/resources/Trump-Pence-Administration-Anti-LGBTQ-Actions-10.21.pdf

Mack, Justin. "Indiana has the second-highest child abuse rate in the nation, report says." *IndyStar*. April 1, 2019.

https://www.indystar.com/story/news/2019/04/01/report-indiana-has-second-highest-child-abuse-rate-nation/3330020002/

Sharry, John. "The importance of relationships and belonging." *The Irish Times*. March 4, 2018.

https://www.irishtimes.com/life-and-style/health-family/parenting/the-importance-of-relationships-and-belonging-1.3405948

Stringer, Kate. "As Indiana's Foster Care Population Rises, New State Data Reveal Troubling Outcomes for Students — but Questions Remain About Whether These Numbers Tell the Whole Story." *The 74 Million*. April 10, 2019.

https://www.the74million.org/article/as-indianas-foster-care-population-rises-new-state-data-reveal-troubling-outcomes-for-students-but-questions-remain-about-whether-these-numbers-tell-the-whole-story/

Zak, A. M., Gold, J. A., Ryckman, R. M., & Lenney, E. (1998). "Assessments of trust in intimate relationships and the self-perception process." *Good Therapy / The Journal of Social Psychology, 138*(2), 217-228. Retrieved from *http://search.proquest.com/docview/199792384?accountid=1229*

About the Authors

Mat Bunch is a social and environmental advocate with a B.S. in Public Policy and is currently pursuing a Master of Public Administration at UNC Chapel Hill. With over a decade of experience in policymaking and energy law, Mat is at the forefront of environmental and social justice. When he is not fighting global climate change during his day job, he enjoys traveling the world and pursuing his mission of inspiring and empowering others to live their true lives, despite their circumstances. He wrote *Wanted* to declare how critical love and belonging are for every soul to flourish.

Candi S. Cross is the founder of You Talk I Write, a modern ghostwriting agency. She has collaborated on 150+ books with authors worldwide. Candi is committed to helping diverse individuals with contemporary stories of impact. She lives in New York City with her wife and 24/7 muse, Liza. For more info, visit *www.youtalkiwrite.com*.

Photo by Liza Andrews

9 789898 505560